HACKNEY SPEEDWAY
FRIDAY AT EIGHT

HACKNEY SPEEDWAY
FRIDAY AT EIGHT

Chris Fenn

TEMPUS

To my wonderful 'Tiger' and 'Crash', I am sorry I have let you down so bad.

*To Thommo, It was those sweeping blasts round the boards that
made it so magical for a nine-year-old.*

To my Bruv, Pete, thanks for taking me in the first place.

To the memory of two Hackney heroes, Dusty Haigh and Vic Harding.

First published 2003

PUBLISHED IN THE UNITED KINGDOM BY:
Tempus Publishing Ltd
The Mill, Brimscombe Port
Stroud, Gloucestershire GL5 2QG

PUBLISHED IN THE UNITED STATES OF AMERICA BY:
Tempus Publishing Inc.
2 Cumberland Street
Charleston, SC 29401

British Library Cataloguing in Publication Data.
A catalogue record for this book is available from the British Library.

ISBN 0 7524 2737 7

Typesetting and origination by Tempus Publishing.
Printed in Great Britain by Midway Colour Print, Wiltshire.

CONTENTS

INTRODUCTION

'Make it a date, Friday at eight' – that was the slogan designed to draw the pre-war crowds to Hackney and was later re-introduced by Hawks promoter Len Silver. Silver invented another slogan too – 'Traxcitement' was coined to describe what you got when you paid your money and walked through the Hackney turnstiles.

When I started going to the Wick as a young boy, speedway was still well supported and it was the highlight of the week for me. We would park along Eastway, there were cars everywhere, and would enter through the turnstiles by the tote board. Once inside I tore at my programme to catch up on news and make sure my favourites were printed in the line-up.

I would quickly make my way to my favourite spot in the stand (a point on the fourth bend) and secure it. In all the years I went to Hackney, apart from the odd race, I never stood anywhere else. To me it was the only place to be and could never understand those on the back straight. Next it was a visit to the track shop. Unbeknown to my mother, during the week I would walk to school and keep the bus fare to spend on souvenirs. Pictures, badges, pennants and patches were added weekly to the collection. Next stop the end of the stand, where the wall was low enough to have a great view into the pits. I would check that all our riders had arrived and wait for the best bit – the smell of burning methanol and the sound of the bikes warming up. There was also a good chance that you may get some autographs in your programme.

Then, at the stroke of eight, back to my spot and waiting for the opening strains of the Hackney theme tune, 'The Magnificent Seven', as the riders walked out for the parade. This was pure ecstasy and the racing had not even started.

I consider myself very lucky to have had Hackney as my local track. Admittedly I am biased, but without doubt many, many people regarded Hackney as the best racing track in the country, if not the world, as it had steep banking and little or no home advantage. Hawks fans were mostly starved of track success but, through it all, the entertainment served up at Waterden Road was second to none. Even through some of Hackney's gravest performances, a splendid time was guaranteed for all. It truly provided traxcitement – a little of which I hope I can recapture here.

The first and last picture of Chris's riding career was taken at the Olle Nygren training school. Shortly after this picture was taken, the throttle jammed open and rider and bike went straight through the King's Lynn safety fence and another promising career was cut short!

ABOUT THE AUTHOR

Chris Fenn started supporting Hackney in 1976 at the tender age of nine. He can still remember his first meeting, the 1976 London Riders Championship, notably for Dave Morton's engine failure, which resulted in Morton kicking his crash helmet away in disgust like a football. Chris fell immediately in love with the sport and has always been grateful to his older brother, Peter, for taking him along on that first night and on many other adventures afterwards.

Chris' childhood hero was Barry Thomas and his proudest speedway moment came when he became Thommo's sponsor in 1988, helping to ensure Hackney's league and cup double that season and also making a small contribution to Thommo achieving the record of riding for the same club for twenty consecutive seasons.

He currently regards himself as fan of the sport in general and prays for the day that speedway returns to his beloved 'Wick'.

Outside speedway, he makes his living laying submarine telecommunications cables, as a senior manager responsible for marine operations. He lives in Kent and has two children, Karen (10) and Adam (6) whom he loves dearly.

ACKNOWLEDGEMENTS

There are so many people that helped me that I should say it's impossible to name them all, but I am going to try anyway. Without the following, this book could never have been written.

The riders: Archie Windmill, Norman Hunter, Tich Read, Trevor Hedge, Jimmy Heard, Colin Pratt, Roy Trigg, Len Silver, Malcolm Brown, Sandy and Jim McGillivray, Bengt Jansson, Laurie Etheridge, Jimmy Gooch, Barry Thomas, Bob Andrews, Eddie Reeves, Graham Miles, Dave Kennett, Zenon Plech, Keith White, Andy Galvin, Mark Loram and Peter Sampson.

The non-riding experts: Robert Andrews, Tony Hurren, John Chaplin, Peter Lipscomb, Chris Illman, Tim Grose, Gary Penfold, Paul Tadman, Terry Stone, Sue Collins, Bryn Williams and Steve Gerwood.

Special thanks go to John Warner and thanks also to Trevor Meeks for providing photographs.

1
THE WICK SPARKS
1935-39

1935 – All Roads Lead To Waterden

Hackney Stadium was built in 1932 to accommodate greyhound racing. It was the stadium owners, Hackney Wick Stadium Ltd, and its managing director, Fred Whitehead, who opened speedway at the Waterden Road circuit in 1935, building a 340-yard circuit inside the dog track. The straights were 31ft wide, with the width at the bends extending to 51ft. There was no banking.

At the end of the 1934 season, the nearby Walthamstow Wolves closed and moved en masse to Hackney and became Hackney Wick Wolves, competing in the National League (then the First Division), which saw teams playing each other home and away twice during the season.

The opening meeting of 1935, complete with capacity crowd.

Fred Evans tosses the coin for gate positions before heat 1, watched by Mick Murphy, Joe Francis, Ron Johnson and Dicky Case.

The team manager was Fred Evans, who had previously been manager at Birmingham, and the team for the first season contained several well-known names, including Dicky Case, Herbert 'Dusty' Haigh, Wally Lloyd, Bill Clibbett, Fred Tate, Mick Murphy and Cyril 'Squib' Burton. Burton had been a spectacular performer, qualifying for the 1931 Star Final. However, his exciting riding ensured that he was dogged by injuries in a career that had encompassed Leicester and Sheffield. His season at Hackney was to prove his last as a rider.

On 26 April, Hackney held a dress rehearsal that today would be called a Press and practice day. Six races took place, featuring Haigh, Clibbett, Tate, Lloyd, Burton, Phil Hart, Reg Stanley, and Clem Thomas. The *Speedway News* reported the track to be a little 'loose and bumpy' and that 'the six-inch white board marking the whole of the inside edge is a positive menace'. They did have room for some praise though, stating that 'the lighting is definitely good and shows to advantage the wide sweeping bends'.

Hackney's first appearance was an away match at New Cross on 1 May 1935, where they were defeated 24-43. Just two days later, on Friday 3 May, Hackney opened to speedway for the very first time with New Cross as the visitors in the return match. The *Speedway News* reported that: 'The whole meeting went through with such zip and sparkle that nineteen races were completed in well under a couple of hours. Well done Hackney, if only for that! That Hackney lost is not surprising for their visitors were the well-experienced New Cross team, who won comfortably by 43-29, but the home side rode a lot better than the score suggests, and if keenness scored points, Hackney would have got a good deal more.'

The paper singled out two men for special praise on that opening night. 'Nevertheless, the man of the match was the Hackney captain Dicky Case, who at the moment must be one of the best men in the country. He won each of his four heats comfortably, but one man cannot make a team and Dick's all-conquering display was all in vain.'

Roy George Arthur Case was born in Toowoomba, Australia. He had come to England in 1930 as a raw twenty year old at the behest of Frank Arthur and was quickly becoming a major force. Having ridden for both Wimbledon and Coventry, Case had finished third in the 1932 Star Riders Championship (the precursor of the World Championship) and became an established test star for Australia.

The other rider to gain a mention in the *Speedway News* was Fred Tate: 'Despite the performances of these familiar riders, the biggest cheer was reserved for Fred Tate, the Hackney reserve. He figured in two races, and although he did not get a place in either, he rode with such dash and grit that he completely captured the crowd. On present form, Tate will soon qualify for a permanent place in the Hackney team.'

The team were beaten again on 7 May, but an improved performance saw them only narrowly beaten at West Ham 34-38. Hackney's first ever win was provided on 10 May,

Hackney's first superstar, Dicky Case, being pushed off for the first ever competitive race at the Wick.

Morian Hansen receives the Distinguished Flying Cross.

beating Harringay at home 40-30, Case was unbeaten and he scored his third successive maximum the following week as Wembley were dispatched 43-28.

During these opening two months, Hackney also contested the ACU Cup against West Ham, Harringay and New Cross, losing all but their final match at home against West Ham. Belle Vue and Wimbledon also won at Waterden Road in the league.

In an effort to strengthen the team, Hackney signed George Wilks from Harringay for the princely sum of £25 and also acquired the services of Danish star Morian Hansen. Murphy and Burton were the two who made way. On coming to England, Hansen had initially ridden for West Ham before joining the Wolves. The move to the Wick was to see the original Great Dane develop into a star name. Hansen was the archetypal all-action tough guy, having also ridden the Wall of Death and taken part in midget car racing. He had been decorated in the Second World War with both the DFC and George Medal.

Monday replaced Friday as race night and on 1 July the mighty Belle Vue made their second appearance of the season. An epic battle saw the match go to a last-heat decider. Drama followed when Max Grosskreutz developed clutch trouble and was excluded under the two-minute rule, before his partner Eric Langton was also excluded for the same offence and Hackney scored a 5-0 to draw.

Cup matches dominated the next two weeks, but there was no good news for the Wolves. Harringay won home and away to knock Hackney out of the National Trophy and West Ham did likewise the following week in the London Cup. Harringay went on to beat West Ham in the London Cup final.

Hackney won their first ever away match at Wimbledon on 27 July, 46-26. With the duck broken, the Wolves also won their next away match, beating New Cross 37-35.

On 24 August Hackney managed to become the only team to win at Belle Vue, securing a 41-30 win. Hackney were without Case, who was on test match duty, but amazingly Belle Vue were without Eric Langton, Joe Abbott and Grosskreutz in the same test and, as if that was not bad enough, Bill Kitchen's car broke down en route and he missed his first ride.

The final meeting of the season saw 'Champions' Belle Vue take on the 'Rest' – which were a team of London captains. Vic Huxley scored 10, leading the London side to a 37-33 victory, with Eric Langton scoring 10 for the Aces.

In their debut season, Hackney finished fifth out of seven in the National League – an acceptable if not brilliant start. Case was undoubtedly the number one. He was nominated to challenge Farndon in the British Individual Championship (match race), but the battles saw a surprising number of falls. At New Cross, Case fell twice as Farndon won 2-0. In the return at Hackney, Case won 2-1, as Farndon fell twice and Case fell once. The decider was held at Wembley and Case fell again as Farndon retained the title 2-1. Case scored five maximums during the year, was the only rider to ride unbeaten all season and he also qualified for his fourth successive Star Final – but would only score 8 points to finish in eighth place in a meeting overshadowed by the previous night's terrible injuries to Tom Farndon which would claim him the following day.

Haigh had ridden well in support and Hansen looked like he would make it to the top. Speedway had arrived at Hackney in great style and this was only the beginning.

SEASON - 1935

20TH MEETING

MONDAY, SEP. 2nd

NATIONAL LEAGUE MATCH

HACKNEY WICK

versus

WIMBLEDON

First Race 8.15 p.m.

Admission 1/3, 1/6 & 2/6 Inc. Tax
Children 7d.

STADIUM SITUATED AT EASTWAY, E.9, BETWEEN LEYTON TOWN HALL AND VICTORIA PARK, HACKNEY

Hackney programme cover, 1935.

1935 National League Record (5/7 teams)

Played	Won	Drawn	Lost	For	Against	Pts
24	10	1	13	824½	879½	21

1935 Cup Record (National Trophy)

Round 1	Harringay	Lost 76-137

1935 League and Cups Points Scorers (captain in italics)

Rider	League	BP	Cup	BP	Total	Maxs
Dicky Case	*207*	*3*	*117*	*3*	*330*	*5*
Dusty Haigh	153½	18	82	5	258½	
Wally Lloyd	108	23	42	8	181	
Bill Clibbett	106	12	42	6	166	
Morian Hansen	74	7	45	2	128	
Fred Tate	57	13	59	8	137	
Cyril Burton	54	7	11	2	74	
Mick Murphy	27	3	16	2	48	
George Wilks	16	5	4	0	25	
Clem Thomas	9	2	7	1	19	
Cliff Parkinson	3	0	9	0	12	
Jack Hobson	10	2	0	0	12	
Phil Hart	0	0	2	0	2	

Leading League CMA

Rider	Mts	Rds	Pts	BP	Total Pts	CMA
Dicky Case	*23*	*84*	*207*	*3*	*210*	*10.00*
Dusty Haigh	22	87	153½	18	171½	7.89

NB Pre-war statistics were badly recorded, with many speedway magazines reporting different figures. There were no CMAs or Bonus Points in those days, only points scored. A group of speedway enthusiasts are currently painstakingly compiling accurate figures and many of these appear here for the first time.

1936 – Tragedy

The following year was to bring mixed fortunes for the Wolves. Case, Hansen, Wilks, Clibbett, Haigh and Tate were retained, but Burton had retired and Lloyd was gone too. In their place were Jack 'Bronco' Dixon and the American Cordy Milne. Milne had been American Champion in 1934 and 1935 and had come to England in 1936 to join New Cross along with his brother, Jack. In an effort to equalise team strengths, the speedway authorities decided that he would ride for Hackney.

The home season commenced on 24 April with a 43-28 league win over West Ham, but Hackney lost their first away match at New Cross on 29 April, 30-39. May again saw the ACU Cup fought out, with Belle Vue replacing New Cross.

As in the previous year, Hackney lost all their matches with the exception of the home tie against West Ham on 15 May. Although they won this encounter, it ended in tragedy for Hackney. Heat 15 saw Dusty Haigh partnered with Bill Clibbett against the Hammers' Tommy Croombs and Ken Brett. As is the case with local derbies, this one had attracted a large crowd and the atmosphere was electric. Dusty gated first and led into the first turn, but fell; the oncoming Croombs and Brett could not avoid him. Dusty was hit by one of the machines and was killed instantly.

Heat 1 riders Fred Tate, Arthur Atkinson, Dicky Case and Tiger Stevenson roar from the tapes in the opening League match of 1936 against West Ham on 24 April. Case won from Atkinson and Stevenson.

The *Speedway News* of 23 May headlined 'A Great Rider Passes On'. The report went on: 'The suddenness of it all was terrible. The race had hardly started before the disaster came. The riders were emerging from the first bend with Haigh slightly ahead. He overslid, and his machine turned half round before he lost control and fell. The fall itself was nothing. His position and close proximity gave the following riders no earthly chance. Mr Fred Whitehead was the first to reach Dusty's side. Dick Case and the rest of the Hackney team streamed across the turf to where their fellow rider lay. They rushed Dusty straight to the ambulance room and thence to hospital but it was no use. The sad news was withheld from the crowd and it was ironic that they left the ground cheering a Hackney victory not knowing one of their stars was dead.'

At the inquest just days later it would be confirmed that Dusty had died instantly from a broken skull. On 20 May a memorial service was held at St John's church, Hackney, to coincide with the funeral at Huddersfield cemetery.

Herbert 'Dusty' Haigh was thirty years old and had previously ridden for Sheffield and Belle Vue before coming to London and joining Lea Bridge, Walthamstow and finally Hackney. Hackney manager Fred Evans took the tragedy particularly badly and he never again became close to one of his riders. Stan Dell took Dusty's place. The tragedy was to cast a shadow over the remainder of the season but the team soldiered on and June was a much better month results-wise for the Wolves. Sadly, there was more bad news to come.

Medical staff prepare to cover the fatally injured Dusty Haigh with a blanket.

The horrifically injured Fred Tate leaves hospital.

June commenced with a break from official action when the Wolves took on 'Putt Mossman's All-Americans'. A record 20,000 crowd saw Hackney win 66-27. The fourteen-and-a-half-stone Bo Lisman gave the Americans their only heat victory when he beat Clibbett in heat 7. Hackney then went on to beat New Cross 116-97 on aggregate to move through the first round of the National Trophy and at West Ham on 30 June they recorded their first away win of the year, winning the league match 44-27.

On 20 June Fred Tate had caused an upset by winning the World Championship qualifying round at Wimbledon. He scored 11 points and Hackney made it a clean sweep when Case and Hansen finished second and third. The second half was a Wimbledon versus Hackney/New Cross challenge match. In heat 7 Tate appeared to touch Case entering a corner and both fell in front of Geoff Pymer who could not avoid them. It was a serious crash that left Tate fighting for his life. He lost an eye and, although it cruelly ended his career, he fortunately pulled through and surgeons managed to rebuild his face using plastic surgery. The Hackney programme notes for the match against Wimbledon on 3 July broke the good news to the Hackney public: 'Supporters will be glad to hear that the critical state of his condition is practically overcome and although it may be a long job he may now come out of his ordeal successfully. Nevertheless, it is only his wonderful courage and splendid physique which have been instrumental in overcoming the terrible nature of his accident. He will be permanently disabled by the loss of one eye, and other facial injuries, and so we very much have to say that he will never ride again.'

Dane Baltzer Hansen (no relation to Morian) was signed to replace Tate. Six days later, on 26 June, Hackney staged a memorial meeting for Haigh. Lionel Van Praag won the meeting with a 15-point maximum from Case on 14 and Bill Pitcher 13.

July saw Hackney's worst run of the year. Although they crushed Wimbledon on 3 July 59-19, they lost the three remaining home matches against New Cross, Belle Vue and Wembley. They did, however, reach the final of the National Trophy, beating Harringay on aggregate 110-105 on successive nights on 17 and 18 July. Hackney did the double again over Harringay on 7 and 8 August, this time in the league.

Fred Evans welcomes Baltzer Hansen to the Wick.

The Hackney team, 1936.

The final of the National Trophy was also held on successive days – 21 and 22 August. The Wolves could not quite pull off a victory, but they shocked the mighty Belle Vue with a 10-point win at home which saw the eclipse of Eric Langton, who only scored 3. The Aces had no trouble pulling back the deficit twenty-four hours later, emerging easy victors 90-122 on aggregate. Case scored a battling 12 but Langton returned to form with 12 and Grosskreutz scored another 18-point maximum, finishing unbeaten throughout the final with a combined 36. Hackney hit back though, and beat New Cross on aggregate 115-97 in the London Cup to move into the final.

On the 10 September the very first World Final was held at Wembley. Hackney provided three finalists, but Lionel Van Pragg won the meeting. Those early finals involved accumulating bonus points in the qualifying rounds. Cordy Milne finished in joint fourth place with Frank Charles, having scored 11 points on the night to add to his 9 bonus points. Just behind in sixth place was team-mate Dicky Case, who finished sixth with 8 points plus 9 bonus points and completing the trio was Morian Hansen, who disappointingly only scored 5 – having gone into the meeting with 10 bonus points – finishing in tenth place. This was the only occasion Hackney would provide three world finalists in the same season.

Hackney finished the campaign with a flourish, doing the double over West Ham and winning away at Wembley, ensuring that the Wolves improved their league position by one place, finishing fourth. They also managed to win their first ever trophy by beating Harringay in the prestigious London Cup, winning both home and away for a 127-88 aggregate victory with Baltzar Hansen scoring 23 points over the two legs.

The strong heat-leader trio of Milne, Case and Hansen was the key to Hackney's improved season. All three scored over 300 points and Case, with 389 points, scored more than any other rider. However, the tragic loss of Haigh took the shine off the season.

1936 National League Record (4/7 teams)

Played	Won	Drawn	Lost	For	Against	Pts
24	11	0	13	855	851	22

1936 Cup Record (National Trophy)

Round 1	New Cross	Won 116-97
Semi-final	Harringay	Won 110-105
Final	Belle Vue	Lost 90-122

1936 League and Cups Points Scorers (captain in italics)

Rider	League	BP	Cup	BP	Total	Maxs
Dicky Case	*203*	*6*	*186*	*2*	*397*	*3*
Cordy Milne	140	19	163	20	342	4
Morian Hansen	179	8	139	15	341	6
George Wilks	87	16	80	18	201	
Bill Clibbett	74	16	61	16	167	
Baltzar Hansen	63	15	69	9	156	
Dusty Haigh	48	2	10	0	60	2
Fred Tate	16	1	39	6	62	
Phil Hart	11	2	31	7	51	
Stan Dell	19	3	10	2	34	
Jack Dixon	14	2	15	0	31	
Jack Hobson	1	0	1	0	2	

Leading League and Cups CMA

Rider	Mts	Rds	Pts	BP	Total	CMA
Dicky Case	40	175	389	8	397	9.07
Cordy Milne	36	164	303	39	342	8.34
Morian Hansen	40	178	318	23	341	7.66

1937 – Dicky Packs His Case

1937 saw Hackney retain their top three – Case, Milne and Hansen – as well as Wilks, Clibbett and Dell, with Ted Bravery replacing Baltzar Hansen.

A challenge match billed as London Champions versus Australians opened the season on 9 April, with Hackney winning 50-34. A poor start to the league campaign followed though, in which Hackney lost their opening three league matches at West Ham and Belle Vue and at home to New Cross (40-42) on 23 April.

Hackney quickly strengthened the team and signed the twenty-two-year-old Australian newcomer Vic Duggan. Hackney won at Wimbledon 44-40 on 26 April and, four days later, Bravery was dropped and replaced by Duggan, who made his debut at Waterden Road but failed to score in Hackney's narrow 42-41 victory over West Ham. Duggan would go on to be one of the post-war years' star names, riding for Harringay and winning the 1948 *Sunday Dispatch* British Riders Final (which was the sport's major competition pending the re-introduction of the World Championship). He missed out on the first post-war World Final in 1949 through injury, but qualified in 1950 and finished in thirteenth place with just 4 points. Sadly his brother Ray was killed, along with Norman Clay, in what remains speedway's only double fatality – a track crash at the Sydney Showground in 1950. Vic was badly affected and retired shortly afterwards.

On 4 June Hackney beat Wimbledon 53-31. Wal Morton – who amazingly would later ride for Hackney as late as 1963 – scored 5 points for the Dons. Hackney and West Ham

A souvenir postcard featuring the 1937 Hackney team. From left to right, top row: Morian Hansen, Cordy Milne, Dicky Case and Stan Dell. Bottom row: Vic Duggan, Bill Clibbett, Fred Evans, George Wilks and Frank Hodgson.

New boys Vic Duggan and Arch Windmill with skipper Dicky Case.

met four times that month in the National Trophy. The first attempt to settle the tie resulted in a 106-106 draw before Hackney went through after winning the replay. During the second leg at West Ham on 29 June, Stan Dell broke his leg. Hackney narrowly lost 53-55, but moved through on aggregate 118-98. Dell was to be dogged by injuries during his career but he kept battling away and also returned after the war to ride as skipper of the Birmingham team. Frank Hodgson replaced Dell and Archie Windmill replaced Clibbett. Dug Wells was also signed.

Hackney met West Ham again in the ACU Cup. The home match was staged on 9 July and, prior to the match, there were three attempts made on the track record by West Ham riders Tiger Stevenson, Eric Chitty and Arthur Atkinson. Nobody could beat Cordy Milne's new record of 70.5, established the week previously in the 43-40 home win over New Cross.

Hackney did not have a good record in the ACU competition and the Wolves also went out of the National Trophy, beaten (as in the previous year's final) by Belle Vue. With both cups falling by the wayside and Hackney's league form being indifferent, retention of the London Cup became the only hope of success. However, that also went astray and West Ham won both legs of the London Cup, winning by a massive 70-146 on aggregate. New Cross went on to beat West Ham in the final.

A never-before-published photograph from Archie Windmill's personal collection shows him chasing his team-mate, World No. 3 Cordy Milne.

The Hackney pits include Joe Abbott and Wally Hull. Interested spectators Tiger Stevenson, Tommy Price and Cliff Parkinson dressed in civvies sit next to Hackney's back row: Ted Bravery, George Greenwood and Fred Whitehead. In front are George Wilks, Dicky Case and Bill Clibbett.

Bill Clibbett falls, Boxing Day 1937.

The World Final was again held at Wembley and Hackney had two finalists. Cordy Milne improved his World Final standing by finishing in third place behind his brother Jack, the new World Champion, and (making it an American whitewash) Wilbur Lamoreaux in second place. Morian Hansen also qualified and finished in eleventh place with 15 points – 8 on the night added to his 7 bonus points.

Hackney slipped one place down the league finishing (as in their debut year) fifth out of seven. Milne and Case again scored over 300 points and, with backing from Hansen, perhaps Hackney should have done better. The home season concluded with an Australians versus Americas challenge match, which the Aussies won 34-37. Dicky Case had decided to retire and the Hackney programme duly sang his praises. He scored 8 points on the night. It was more than just Case that Hackney would say goodbye to.

1937 National League Record (5/7 teams)

Played	Won	Drawn	Lost	For	Against	Pts
24	10	0	14	935½	1,062½	20

1937 Cup Record (National Trophy)

Round 1	West Ham	Draw 106-106
Round 1	West Ham	Won 118-98 (replay)
Semi-final	Belle Vue	Lost 95-121

1937 League and Cups Points Scorers (captain in italics)

Rider	League	BP	Cup	BP	Total	Maxs
Cordy Milne	222	3	147	2	374	5
Dicky Case	*180*	*11*	*134*	*0*	*325*	
Morian Hansen	182	1	102	3	288	1
George Wilks	106½	23	60	10	199½	
Bill Clibbett	68	11	41	11	131	
Vic Duggan	50	9	30	9	98	
Stan Dell	42	8	21	3	74	
Frank Hodgson	38	8	13	5	64	
George Greenwood	10	3	14	1	28	
Dug Wells	12	5	1	0	18	
Ted Bravery	11	2	2	1	16	
Archie Windmill	8	1	1	0	10	

Leading League and Cups CMA

Rider	Mts	Rds	Pts	BP	Total	CMA
Cordy Milne	36	160	369	5	374	9.35
Dicky Case	*35*	*152*	*314*	*11*	*325*	*8.55*
Morian Hansen	36	156	284	4	288	7.38

1938 – Wolves Triumphant

As a result of falling gates, the Hackney management decided that a change of race night from Friday to Saturday may help stem the tide. However, with objections from Harringay (who likewise ran on Saturdays in the first division) Hackney would have to compete in the second division to achieve their goal. To mark their transition, a new second division track record would be recorded and the club colours were also changed from black and white to champagne and claret.

With Case gone, it also meant that other star riders, Milne and Hansen, would also have to leave and both joined Bristol. Case would later change his mind about retirement and join Wembley along with Wilks, who was transferred for £350 – a nice profit on the initial £25 investment. Duggan also left and joined Bristol. Frank Hodgson was the new captain. He had joined Hackney in 1935, working behind the scenes as a sign-writer before deciding to try his luck at speedway in 1937. Joining him were Dug Wells, Stan Dell and Arch Windmill and, completing the main squad, were Jim Baylais, Tommy Bateman and Jack Tidbury.

The season commenced with the English Speedway Trophy. Having lost at Birmingham on 13 April, Hackney won their opening four home matches against Wembley reserves, Birmingham, New Cross and Norwich. Sadly, Stan Dell was injured again during a second-half event at West Ham on 26 April. Coincidentally, he broke the same leg by falling in the same place two years running, having not ridden at West Ham between those dates. George Saunders would replace him.

On 17 May the National Trophy qualifying round was held at Nottingham and Hackney succumbed 48-60. The second leg took place four nights later and Hackney just failed to pull back the deficit, winning on the night 59-49 and thereby going down by 2 points on aggregate. Nottingham later pulled out of the league and the result was expunged, reinstating Hackney and giving them a second chance against Leeds – which they took, winning on aggregate 122-92.

The next round followed closely with Birmingham as the opponents and, despite an 8-point deficit from the first leg, Hackney moved through to the final, winning 66-42 on 18 June. Hackney completed June by winning their first National League Second Division match, 58-26 against Newcastle. July saw Norwich finally knock Hackney out of the

A Hackney programme from 1938.

Action from Hackney against New Cross Reserves on 23 July 1938 in the English Speedway Trophy. The Wolves won 49-35.

National Trophy in the qualifying round final by winning on aggregate 94-121. The matches were held on 2 and 9 July and, to complete a trio of wins in successive weeks, Norwich won 28-55 on 16 July at home in the English Speedway Trophy. In the league the news was better. Despite defeats at Wolves, Sheffield and Southampton, Hackney won at Newcastle and Leeds before again losing to West Ham reserves – ironically nicknamed the 'Hawks' – on 5 August.

The English Speedway Trophy was completed with another home loss the following night when Southampton won at the Wick 38-43. Stan Dell returned to action in this match, but could only manage 3 points. Southampton won the Southern section of the competition by a clear 6 points, with Hackney in second place. The winners of the Northern section, Belle Vue, went on to beat Southampton in the final.

The Wolves hit back from this disappointment though by winning at Lea Bridge in the league 46-37, before Norwich knocked them out of the Provincial Trophy 95-119 on aggregate. However, Hackney would have the last laugh over Norwich.

The first test match ever to be staged at Hackney was held on 3 September. Hackney had four riders selected and, to mark the occasion, the management struck a special medal for their riders, which was presented prior to the meeting by Bluey Wilkinson. The Hackney scorers were Wells 12, Hodgson 5, Dell 4 and Windmill 0. England lost to the Dominions 40-67; Vic Duggan 18 and Bluey Wilkinson 17½ were both unbeaten.

Charlie Appleby pulls on helmet colour whilst Norwich's Max Grosskreutz watches. Sitting behind them, Tommy Bateman (smoking) gives advice to Stan Dell and Archie Windmill (standing) during the Provincial trophy match on 20 August. Dug Wells' attention is elsewhere!

Hackney moved into league title contention when they beat Norwich 48-35 at Waterden Road on 17 September and then won at Birmingham 46-37 four days later. Having been crushed at Norwich on 24 September 26-55, the Wolves trailed Norwich by 4 match points with two matches in hand and all four remaining matches at home. Southampton and Sheffield were both beaten and Hackney were level with Norwich on 20 points each, but Hackney were ahead on race points, leading by 28 points.

Both teams raced their penultimate matches on 15 October. Norwich thrashed Sheffield 63-21 and Hackney beat Birmingham 57-27, closing the gap on race points to 22. The championship deciders were held on 22 October. Norwich took on lowly Birmingham, looking to score as many points as possible, and Hackney took on neighbours Lea Bridge knowing that 49 points would be enough to make the title theirs.

The battle went to the penultimate race when Archie Windmill led home his partner Jack Tidbury for a 5-1, putting the Wolves on 50 points; the championship was theirs for the first time in the team's history. In anticipation, the trophy had been brought to the Wick and was presented to Frank Hodgson whilst fireworks erupted overhead and the huge crowd went crazy. Movie cameras recorded the celebrations, although the short film 'Flying Cinders' pretended that the final race had decided the championship.

Hackney's League-winning team. From left to right: Ken Brett (wearing helmet),
Charlie Appleby, Jack Tidbury, Archie Windmill, Stan Dell, Frank Hodgson, Charlie
Page (hidden), George Saunders, Jim Baylais, Tommy Bateman, Dug Wells and Fred
Evans.

Hackney won the match 51-33 with Wells unbeaten on 12, Windmill 11, Hodgson 10
and solid backing from Baylais 6, Dell 5, Stock 4, Tidbury 2 and Saunders 1. Norwich
beat Birmingham 63-21, losing the championship by 10 race points.

The top three had been superb. Wells was unbeaten in the last three league matches
whilst Hodgson was a superb captain and Windmill provided excellent backing.
Hackney and speedway in general was looking in good shape, but nobody could
foresee the horrors about to unfold.

1938 National League Division Two Record (1/9 teams)

Played	Won	Drawn	Lost	For	Against	Pts
16	12	0	4	759	574	24

1938 Cup Record (National Trophy, Qualifying)

Round 1	Nottingham	Lost 107-109
		(result expunged)
Round 2	Leeds	Won 122-92
Semi-final	Birmingham	Won 115½-99½
Final	Belle Vue	Lost 94-121

1938 League and Cups Point Scorers (captain in italics)

Rider	League	Cup	Total	Maxs
Dug Wells	150	170	320	10
Frank Hodgson	*149*	*164½*	*313½*	7
Archie Windmill	86	137	223	3
George Saunders	86	77	163	
Jim Baylais	80	100	180	1
Jack Tidbury	60	62	122	
Tommy Bateman	39	73	112	1
Stan Dell	52	58	110	1
Nobby Stock	33	–	33	
Ken Brett	11	11	22	
Charlie Appleby	13	6	19	

1939 – Riders Go AWOL

In an attempt to retain their title, the Wolves re-signed another top name in ex-Birmingham captain Phil 'Tiger' Hart, who had ridden briefly for Hackney in 1936. Hodgson would again lead the side with Windmill, Wells, Dell, Saunders and Baylais all retained. Nobby Stock, known as the 'Flying Milkman', and Ken Brett completed the squad.

It was action all the way in April when the English Speedway Trophy got into full swing against Norwich, Crystal Palace and Bristol. Hackney won their home matches and also away at Bristol, but Norwich only lost one match and topped the table. In the last away match at Crystal Palace on 29 May, Hackney had a great opportunity to qualify on race points but lost the match narrowly 40-43, despite losing skipper Hodgson with a hand injury. Before that, Hackney disposed of Stoke in the National Trophy qualifying round, winning 119-96 on aggregate. Hackney were well beaten in the second leg 39-68, but had a massive lead from the first leg when they had won by 80-28.

In the league, the Wolves won their three opening home matches against Stoke, Newcastle and Bristol, but lost their opening away match at Bristol. The home match

Frank Hodgson buckles his race-jacket next to a laughing Jack Tidbury.

The distinctive style of Hackney's Windmill.

against Bristol was held on 27 May and, prior to Hackney's 53-29 win, Vic Duggan returned and beat Hodgson in a special match race.

To the crowd's excitement, Dicky Case was re-signed to replace the injured Hodgson and he made his first Hackney appearance of the year in the World Championship qualifying round on 3 June. Wembley's Andy Menzies won the meeting with 14 points, with home stars Windmill and Saunders in second and third places. Sadly, Case fell in his first ride and, although he rode and won his second ride, he then retired from the meeting – ending a very premature comeback. Outside of the Rye House training school he later ran, he never rode again.

On 10 June, Middlesbrough came to Waterden Road and ran Hackney very close. A last heat from Saunders and Windmill gave Hackney a 44-40 victory. Sadly, shortly afterwards Middlesbrough closed down and the result was deleted from the records. It did, however, hand Hackney a seeded place in the final of the National Trophy.

For the second successive season, Hackney staged a test match against Dominions. On 24 June, despite tracking four Hackney riders, England were defeated 40-67. Wolves' scorers were Baylais 9, Hart 7, Windmill 3 and Dell 0. Middlesbrough's George Greenwood top-scored for England with 13, whilst Dominions' top riders were Jimmy Gibb, who scored an unbeaten 18-point maximum, Ernie Evans 16 and Eric Chitty 15.

Hackney won their three home league matches in July – against Stoke, Bristol and Newcastle – but it was to be Sheffield's month, as they won three of their four matches with Hackney. The final of the qualifying round for the National Trophy was first. Hackney won the home leg on 8 July 67-39, thanks to the return of Hodgson. The return leg was staged five days later and Hackney were thrashed 33-75 to lose on aggregate by 14 points. A fortnight later and the teams were at it again, this time in the Provincial Trophy. Hackney lost both legs to lose by an aggregate score of 73½-115½. Hodgson was injured again in the first leg at Sheffield on 27 July, this time with a broken toe, and in the return match two days later, Saunders broke his collarbone. He did not ride for Hackney again as he was called up for military service.

With the political climate in Europe heading for crisis, August saw any hope of Hackney retaining their title receive serious setbacks. Without Hodgson and Saunders, they lost away league matches at Belle Vue and Norwich and even on Hodgson's return the match at Bristol was lost. The Union Cup also commenced and Hackney beat Norwich and Bristol at Waterden Road before losing at Norwich. This competition, like the league championship, would never be completed.

England declared war on Germany on 3 September and the season was brought to a premature end. Hackney were in second place in the league when hostilities broke out, but were 6 points adrift of leaders Newcastle and it looked unlikely that they would have retained their title. The Second World War was to rage for six years. On its conclusion speedway slowly returned to normal and tracks around the country started to open again. This was not the case at Hackney Wick, however, and it was to be close to a quarter of a century before the roar returned to Waterden Road.

1939 National League Division Two Record (2/6 teams pre-war)

Played	Won	Drawn	Lost	For	Against	Pts
13	7	0	6	567	512	14

1939 Cup Record (National Trophy, Qualifying)

Round 1	Stoke	Won 119-96
Semi-final	Middlesborough	Walk Over
Final	Sheffield	Lost 100-114

1939 League and Cups Points Scorers (captain in italics)

Rider	League	Cup	Total	Maxs
Jim Baylais	114	122	236	6
Frank Hodgson	77	*132*	*209*	8
Archie Windmill	85	98	183	3
Dug Wells	59	72½	131½	5
Stan Dell	48	81	129	1
Phil Hart	54	69	123	2
Nobby Stock	58	62	144	
George Saunders	42	66	108	
Ken Brett	18	12	30	

HACKNEY HERO
ARCHIE WINDMILL

Spider Spins A Yarn

Archie Windmill is one of the last of Hackney's pre-war heroes. He originally rode grass-track and became a member of the famous Barnet grass-track club, where he was spotted by Australia's very first World Champion, Lionel Van Praag. He recalls: 'Actually I started racing on the grass-track at Barnet speedway and I was doing well then and was very friendly with Lionel Van Praag of Wembley and used to see him quite often. I'd only got an old Rudge engine but he said to me "I've got an old Jap here" and he said that he'd used it in the London Riders Championship. "It's not bad" he said and "you can use that if you like" and I won the South Midland Centre Championship. I did not know at the time, but that automatically gave you a contract with a London club. I did not know which club, but it turned out to be Hackney speedway and that's how I got started.'

Archie went on to be one of Hackney's leading pre-war riders and was a vital part of the 1938 league-winning team. He represented his country against the Dominions before war intervened to bring his career to a temporary end. 'I still hold the old Hackney Track, four-lap record because during the war it was bombed and after it was a slightly different size – so I shall hold that record for ever.'

What about the riders Archie had ridden with? 'George Wilks was my best mate – both being hard up, we won races. The best Hackney rider was Cordy Milne, but he was not a team rider. He said to me "I am over here and I want to win" so I was always racing three blokes, but it was all right because it got me more points. I partnered both Morian Hansen and Cordy Milne. I was in match races with Fay Taylour. She passed me once. It was harder than the ordinary league racing, the ACU would not let them ride though. When Vic Duggan come over he signed at the same time as me. He was quite good. At Halifax, I was scratching for points having a hell of a time. Vic was there and he said "you know what you're doing wrong, well it's banked and you are driving down the straight like you do at Hackney, shutting off at the corner and then opening up round the corner", he said "shut off halfway down the straight and drive the corners". I plucked up courage next time out and started winning races and that was old Vic he could weigh things up like that.

'I rode with Putt Mossman, the American. During the interval he always gave a bit of a show and one week they put up a wooden gantry with a little run-up to it and he had an Indian motorbike and was going to go through it. They had knocked the nails into the wood so that, as he hit, the wood would slide off. Well, what Dicky Case, Cordy Milne and the others done was hammered the nail over. The Indian bike would not start so he said "I'm not disappointing my public" and he decided to use my speedway bike. So he went across the grass getting up a bit of speed, well you know it was like hitting a brick wall. The front wheel was back past the engine, but he went through it and broke the wood!

'On another occasion he rode from a ramp in the grandstand roof into a tank of petrol but crashed and broke his nose. The trouble there was that it had rained. They told him but he was like that. He was a boy that Mossman, he had a big Cadillac, pure white and it was covered all over in women's names and address. He had a ladder on the Indian bike and he used to set the throttle and climb the ladder and down the other side and then back again.

'Dicky Case was captain of Hackney and we had Belle Vue down. I went in the afternoon to the workshop to get some things done on the bike and Dicky Case was there and he said "Come with me". We went out onto the track and up to the tapes. He pulled the tapes down and where the best grip was he pencil-marked the tapes. He said "When tonight comes you get your front wheel on the mark and you'll be away".

But what we didn't know was the Eric Langton, the captain of Belle Vue, had come early and was watching us from the stand. When we went, he took the tape mark out and marked it up wrong. I liked Dicky Case: he was a wild man but good natured and not dangerous.

'I liked Morian too, he would always help you. If you thought a position on the starting line was better he would readily swap with you. A lot of the others wouldn't. Cordy Milne would always just choose what he wanted, but that just made me ride harder. At Hackney, gates 2 and 4 were the best – but I liked 2. Old Morian was a peaceable bloke normally, but this night he got trouble with the bike and when we came in the pits he took his helmet off and – I'd never seen this done before – he got hold of the bike by the tube under the saddle and the front fork,

Speedway rider and stuntman Putt Mossnam on his Indian!

lifted it above his head and threw it against the wall. I could never lift one on my own, but he was a strong bloke. There was a rider called Baltzer Hansen (no relation to Morian); he couldn't speak a word of English. They fixed him up with a car and up the road in Hackney High Street he hit a milk float so they sent for Morian to interpret for him, but Morian thought he would have some fun and said all the wrong things and the police put Baltzer in the cells for the night. Well, three nights later Baltzer was round the stadium with a revolver and told everyone he was gonna get Morian and shoot him! For a dare, Morian once drove his car up the steps in the grandstand to get his car near the clubhouse and, on another occasion, I was with him and we were going down the road and there was about twelve or fifteen bikes – cyclists riding side by side, or three abreast. Well old Morian had to wait, he blew the hooter but they just kept going. When he did get by he roared past and went round in front and slammed the brakes on. He had a trailer on with two bikes and they all piled up on the ground with all these bikes everywhere!'

What was the club and management like? 'Hackney was very good for its surface and the set-up was good: a good clubhouse, a good stadium and a good workshop and they would help you there. In the pits you always had your place allocated. They paid travel money too. The trouble though was the amount of foreign riders, they kept moving about but the English riders stayed loyal. If the Hackney team had kept together then we would have won more and challenged the likes of Wembley, but the team was broken up and then the war came. My best years were with Hackney, I had some bloody good times there. An average wage was £5 a week, but I could make myself £100 a week. There was bags of crumpet too!

'Fred Evans and Fred Whitehead were both nice men. When the war broke out I could have gone with Whitehead as a dispatch rider, but went into the Air Force at Harlesdon. I wish I had become a dispatch rider though, as I could have ridden with all the others at Belle Vue. A lot of the riders went into the munitions factories. I ended up flying Tiger Moths and Wellingtons and finished up in the a Lancaster squadron, but ended up being pulled out because I was partially colour-blind. Stan Dell and I were a formidable pair. He leg-trailed and I rode foot forward. Often we would nip smartly out the gate and just stick together and so they left us like that as a pairing. I was always with Stan – Fred Evans was clever like that.'

So what now would be good for speedway? 'Hackney had crowds queuing up in the afternoon – it was absolutely packed and you could not get in sometimes. The trouble with the riders today is they don't go and mix with the crowd. They should bring cinders back, you could pass somebody on cinders, although I don't know if you can get it these days.' After the war, Archie was allocated to Wimbledon and later moved on to Walthamstow. Currently he is the president of the Veteran Dirt-track Riders Association and still takes an active interest in speedway racing today. Archie was the type of speedway rider that the sport is dependent on. He cares about it passionately and also for the crowd he entertained. With the war disrupting a promising career, he was in the wrong place at the wrong time, yet he has obviously enjoyed life to the full and speedway has been lucky that he crossed its path.

The Case of Fred Evans

In the late 1990s, speedway fan and former grass-track rider Chris Illman was browsing in a junk shop in Greenwich. He spotted a battered old case and glanced inside to see a lot of old papers, but also a couple of old speedway photographs. Trying not to seem too keen in case the price escalated, he quickly closed the case and agreed a deal with the shop owner to buy the case for £10. What he did not know when he left the shop was that the case contained a speedway treasure trove.

The case had belonged to Hackney's pre-war team manager, Fred Evans, and it contained his personal effects. These included his passport (giving his birthday as 27 July 1901), his wallet with money still inside and cheques made out in the names of pre-war Hackney stars, share certificates and car registration and tax documents. The mystery is how Fred came to be separated from his case. The last dated document inside it is *The Times* newspaper from Saturday 26 August 1939, which lists the Territorial Army officers and includes Fred's name. Although this is pure supposition, the case appears to have been packed up for the war and never collected from where it was stored. Following the suspension of speedway season, Fred joined the territorial reserves. However, little is known about Fred Evans after the war. He became team manager at Norwich and it is rumoured that he eventually became a publican. It is also believed that Fred remained single throughout his life as many of the invitations are to 'Fred Evans and Girls'.

Among the case's more interesting Hackney effects are more than 100 photographs of Hackney riders, team photographs and even pictures of the track being built. These pictures are of huge historical value.

Disappointingly, Fred's diaries do not add much to the story. Two diaries are in the case (for 1937 and 1938). They contain information on Hackney riders' appearances at other tracks and other appointments. The diaries are completed in pencil but the most poignant entry is that for 16 May 1937, which being the only entry written in pen simply says '1st Anniversary Dusty Haigh'. There is also an invitation to the reception of Cordy Milne's wedding to Willis von Schaach. The reception was held at Hackney Stadium on 25 July 1936. Also in the case are his speedway passes, letter of engagement as speedway manager at Birmingham and many newspaper clippings – all contain Fred's name clearly marked out in pencil.

Other items shed some light on his personal life. Whilst manager at Hackney he lived in the White Hart Hotel on Hackney Marshes and was a member of the Chorley Wood golf club. He owned a greyhound called 'Whatnot' and, as war loomed, he was in the process of opening a new speedway at Ramsgate in which he invested £100. No doubt there is much more to the Fred Evans story, which so far remains lost. If anybody knows what happened to Fred, the custodian of his memories would love to hear from you.

Chris Illman (right) shows the secret's of Fred's case to the author Chris Fenn (left) and surviving rider from the Evans era, Archie Windmill (centre). Windmill recalls that the last time he saw the case was when Evans was loading it into the back of his car over sixty-five years ago.

The case.

2
THE WICK ROARS
1963-69

1963 – Foot Forward

By 1962, the halcyon days of speedway had long gone and London was reduced to just one track at Wimbledon. It was a different world. Cinder tracks and spectacular leg-trailing had gone, along with crowds measured in the tens of thousands. Now it was shale tracks and the bikes were Japs and Jawas.

Fred Whitehead was still managing director at Hackney Stadium and had always been keen to reintroduce speedway. During the winter of 1963/64, Mike Parker (who had promoted at venues around the country and was at the time the current promoter at both Leicester and Bradford) decided that the crowds at these two venues were simply not sufficient to continue and decided to bring Provincial League speedway to London. This was a large gamble as the Provincial League was very much seen as the lower division and of course speedway had not been seen at Waterden Road for so long. A public meeting was held in January 1963 and approximately 100 fans braved the cold weather to hear the news that Hackney was to return.

Wednesday was the new race night and, on 10 April 1963, the roar of the engines was heard once more at Waterden Road on the new, but very bumpy, 345-yard track. The challenge match visitors to open the new era were New Cross, the team that rode in the very first match at Hackney in 1935. The team were now called the Hawks and the match finished as a draw, 38-38.

The 1963 starting line-up was a mixture of youth and experience led by the new skipper Norman Hunter: 'My first team was at Leicester with Mike Parker. They closed down and so I went to Hackney. I worked there during the winter helping to build the track and I was the first person to ride the track. I wanted that honour since I had helped build it.' Joining him were Trevor Hedge, John Poyser and Pete Sampson, backed by veteran Ipswich fence-scraper Tich Read and pre-war star Wal Morton who, at around fifty years of age, would be the oldest rider ever to wear a Hackney race-jacket. Alec Ford was the team manager.

Coronation Street actor Kenneth Cope performed the opening ceremony and Tommy Sweetman won the opening race in a time of 75.8, but Hunter had reduced the record to 73.6 by the end of the meeting. Sweetman was a guest for former World number three Jack Biggs, whose name appeared in the programme but had decided to join Coventry instead. It would be a further four years before Biggs finally lined up in a

Trevor Hedge had two spells riding for Hackney, in 1963 and 1976.

'Wrecker' Jimmy Heard.   *Pete Sampson.*

Hackney race-jacket. Unknown New Zealander Colin McKee was Biggs' permanent replacement and made his debut the following week at New Cross.

A series of Southern league matches followed, but Hackney struggled and finished second from bottom in the five-team tournament that also featured (last place) Rayleigh, New Cross, Exeter and (champions) Poole. It was obvious that the Hawks would need strengthening, as Hunter was clearly carrying the team. Parker tried and failed to sign Reg Trott, but he eventually secured Jimmy Heard from Stoke, who replaced Wal Morton. Heard had started like many of that time in cycle speedway, riding for the Stratford Hammers. Having ridden alongside Len Silver at Stratford, he later found himself at the same Egyptian air force base and riding on Silver's homemade desert speedway track. His first speedway track was at Rye House in the Southern Area League, before moving on the Eastbourne and latterly Stoke.

'Hedgey was only a youngster then and we rode at Exeter and he brought his girlfriend with him. After the meeting we didn't see anything of him. So we all went down to St Austell for the Tuesday night, dumped our bikes in the pits and decided to go down to the beach; Pete Sampson, Colin McKee, Norman Hunter and I decided to get this boat out and who should we run into but Trevor and his girlfriend out in the middle of the bay. So we started filling his boat up with water – but his girlfriend couldn't swim. She was worried that we were going to sink his boat.'

Injuries were to play an important part and the Hawks lost both Poyser (with a broken wrist) and Sampson (broken leg). This gave a chance to a young man who had been riding in second-half races called Malcolm Simmons. Simmons was to go on to be one of England's best riders and finish second in the 1976 World Championship. His career was often shrouded in controversy and he returned to ride for Hackney again twenty-three years later.

Rider changes were to continue throughout the season. Ronnie Rolfe was signed in May in time for the first Provincial League match, which was held on 10 May against the victorious Southern League Champions, Poole. They had won at the Wick earlier in the season 33-45, but after a superb performance this time Hackney emerged as 44-34 winners.

The Hawks' Provincial League campaign produced little on their travels and most of the time they were easily beaten – sometimes heavily, including a 23-53 defeat at Edinburgh and an 18-60 thrashing at Poole. They won most of their home matches though, including a narrow victory over Wolverhampton, 40-38, where the original blond bombshell Graham Warren scored 11 points from four rides, being beaten only in heat 1 by Norman Hunter. Tich Read bowed out for the remained of the year after sustaining concussion for the umpteenth time in July.

'A rough old time I had there because the track was as rough as hell. Several times I went over the top and got hooked up in the fence. I went back to Norwich but I was too committed with business and it was too much with the travelling. All the bloody pile-ups put a dampener on things.'

That same month Colin Pratt, a rider destined to play a significant part in Hackney's future, led Stoke to victory at Hackney on 17 July by 34-43, Pratt scoring 9 paid 11.

The season played out in much the same way and Hackney finished in tenth place out of thirteen in their opening Provincial League campaign – a good performance from the opening season. Hunter was the star of the season, achieving what no pre-war Hackney rider had been able to do by becoming the first Hackney rider to win the prestigious London Riders Championship. Trevor Hedge and Malcolm Simmons were the season's other success stories, with Hedge improving throughout the season and winning the Stadium Directors' Trophy. Simmons, meanwhile, in his first year, was clearly showing what potential he had.

The programme for the last meeting of the season on 2 October, against a side labelled as 'The Rest', carried a tribute to former World Champion Peter Craven, who had lost his life as a result of a track crash at Edinburgh. In his programme notes Mike Parker wrote: 'While the team have not won any trophies this season, I am sure that you will agree that they have given a very good account of themselves. The average age of tonight's Hawks squad is under twenty-one, that makes them just about the youngest league side ever in the sport.' Hackney was back and the man that started it all back in 1935, Fred Whitehead, could not contain his delight and, also in the season's final programme, confirmed that: 'My personal ambition to revive speedway racing at our stadium has at long last been realised.'

1963 Provincial League Record (10/13 teams)

Played	Won	Drawn	Lost	For	Against	Pts
24	10	1	13	875	990	21

1963 Cup Record

Round 1	Bye	
Round 2	Home v. New Cross	Won 54-42
Semi-final	Away v. Newcastle	Lost 36-60

1963 Provincial League Averages (captain in italics)

Rider	Mts	Rds	Pts	BP	Total	CMA
Norman Hunter	*22*	*94*	*229*	*7*	*236*	*10.04*
Trevor Hedge	22	84	130	9	139	6.62
Jimmy Heard	24	95	141	14	155	6.52
Colin McKee	20	81	112	19	131	6.47
Tich Read	11	40	48	9	57	5.70
Malcolm Simmons	18	68	79	12	91	5.35
John Poyser	6	23	24	2	26	4.52
Peter Sampson	15	45	46	4	50	4.44
Wal Morton	12	35	30	3	33	3.77
Ronnie Rolfe	10	35	27	5	32	3.66

[Brian Davies 1.67 (5 matches only)]

1964 – The Year Of The Black

During the close season, a major disagreement broke out between the promoters of the Provincial League and the National League. The result was that the Speedway Control Board (SCB) outlawed the Provincial League, which meant that, officially, this season never took place!

West Ham was re-opening but this row was to deprive both teams of local rivalry as West Ham joined the 'official' National League. It also had a devastating effect on the Hackney team as many riders concerned about falling foul of the authorities moved on to pastures new. Malcolm Simmons left to join West Ham, but worse still skipper Norman Hunter went with him – taking many supporters too.

'I left because of the year of the black, but I wanted to make something of myself and didn't feel I could do that in the Provincial League. I wanted to ride in the National League where the second strings were equivalent to PL heat leaders.'

Trevor Hedge and Tich Read both returned to parent club Norwich and Colin McKee joined Oxford. With Sampson out with a lef injury sustained whilst playing football and Heard hospitalised with appendicitis, the Hawks were left with two juniors, John Poyser and Brian Davies, and the major task of rebuilding a team.

Several strange Hackney line-ups took to the track in the opening meetings. Heavy defeats at Wolves and Poole in the Southern League saw Hackney track what essentially were a team of guests. Maury McDermott top scored with 10 points in the 25-53 drubbing at Exeter, whilst Ron Bagley, Pete Jarmen and Clive Featherby scored the bulk of the points at Poole in the 33-45 defeat. Dennis Day made his debut in these matches, having been signed from Exeter. Amazingly, a superb team was assembled and when the home season opened against Exeter on 29 April, Mike Parker was adamant that the campaign would be a good one, stating: 'What's become of the Hackney Hawks? All the riders have left the team and gone to that other league, we won't have a decent team and no chance at all in the league. These, and a few more, are the rumours that have been flying about these last few weeks. NONSENSE. Hackney will have a team that will compare with any in the league.'

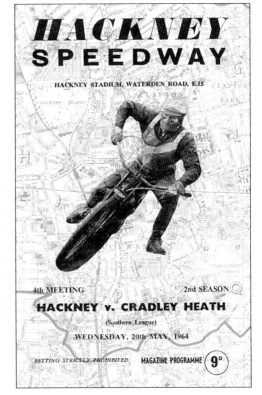

1964 programme.

Colin Pratt had been signed from Stoke, Roy Trigg joined from Wimbledon. Both had made their debuts in the 27½-49½ away defeat at Long Eaton on 28 April. Trigg had had several second-half races at New Cross and Rye House before being snapped up by Wimbledon in 1962. He was loaned to Poole and helped them to win the Provincial League. He was recalled to Wimbledon in 1963, but the dispute between the two leagues saw him sign for Hackney. He recalls: 'The first meeting I had at Hackney was on my twenty-first birthday on 29 April. I was the first guy to go "black". Bob Andrews did it and they served him with a writ but I was under twenty-one and my father had been ill and he had not countersigned it.' Hackney beat Newport 44-34 in the Southern League on 6 May and Parker's team-building plans were still being completed: 'Further to my mike announcement last week, I hope to have Exeter 'big gun' Len Silver in our line-up within a few weeks. As soon as we can arrange a replacement for Len at Exeter he will become another new 'Hawk'. Len will also have an interest in the promotion side here at Hackney and should be a tremendous asset to us all.' That would turn out to be a major understatement.

Rayleigh star Les McGillivray was persuaded to come out of retirement in what was to be another major turning point for the club. Known as 'Atom Bomb', McGillivray started racing at Rayleigh in 1948 when he was only seventeen years old. He also saw service at Ipswich, Coventry and Poole. In 1962 he had a bad crash with Cyril Brine at Wimbledon and was paralysed down one side. But, typically, he fought back to health and returned to Rayleigh in 1963. He made his Hackney debut at Exeter on 4 May in the 26-52 defeat.

Les McGillivray, one of Hackney's most reliable riders.

Hackney 1964. From left to right: Roy Trigg, John Poyser, Brian Davies, Alec Ford, Dennis Day, Les McGillivray, Len Silver. Colin Pratt is seated on the bike.

Silver joined shortly afterwards, scoring 11 points on his debut at home to Cradley in the home Southern League match on 20 May. Having finished in fifth place in the Southern League, the Hawks began to win both home and away, including victories at Wolverhampton and Poole, where Les McGillivray's brother Sandy made his debut, scoring 3 points. In an effort to stop falling gates, the 12 June saw Hackney revert to the original pre-war race night of Friday at eight o'clock, putting a gap between Hackney and the Tuesday night meetings at West Ham. But times were still hard as Trigg recalls:

'Silver approached us and said he wanted us to travel together to reduce expenses. We had a tour to Middlesbrough and then Edinburgh and he arranged for a car with a trailer on the back. We had seven bikes in the trailer and five of us in a four-seater Morris Oxford. When we got on the A1 we got our foot down and the trailer started swinging out of sync. Next thing someone said "Hey someone's bikes have fallen off", Pratt said "If that's my bike I'm going home". He was cursing. He stopped and these two bikes were propped up on the middle of the A1 with lorries driving round them.

'Hackney's mechanic was the late Alec Mosley. Alec was a top class engine tuner that Len brought in to sort out anyone who needed help with their motors, and I for one had a real change in fortune when he took me onboard. His "workshop" was in an upstairs bedroom of his home and you had to carry your engine up the stairs for him as, due to health problems, he couldn't do any lifting. All in this small bedroom he had a lathe, a boring bar, valve-seat cutting machine, pillar drills – you name it, he had it! When he had stripped the engine down he would give the crankcases to his wife and she would set to and wirebrush the outsides of the crankcases until they shone. She used to use a brand new brush for each engine! When you put in an engine after it had been to Alec, the opposition riders in the pits used to think you had a brand new engine in your bike. In the first season I was with Alec, I didn't have one engine failure because of his work!'

Hackney's next away success came in very controversial circumstances. They visited Cradley on 20 June and won 42-36 with a superb maximum from Pratt. Len Silver had to have police protection to leave the stadium, having been blamed for a crash by home rider Johnny Hart. Despite being cleared by the referee, some Cradley supporters took matters into their own hands and attempted to lynch Len. Blows were exchanged in a rare example of speedway crowd trouble. It was only to get worse for Silver though.

On 3 July he crashed in heat 5 of the cup match against his former club, Exeter, and broke his wrist and collarbone. His career as a rider was over. Amazingly, despite this setback Hackney did the double over the much-fancied Newcastle, who tracked Ivan Mauger in their line-up, winning at home 42 -36 on 17 July and away 41-37 three days later. Even that was not to be enough though. Away defeats at Sheffield and Glasgow were the catalyst to just missing out on the Provincial League title.

In a break from league racing, Hackney staged their first post-war test match on 12 August when Britain beat an Overseas team 58-50. Newport was going to be Hackney's bogey team for the year. They had managed a draw at Hackney and thrashed the Hawks in the return 27-51, where Trigg managed to score 15 of Hackney's meagre tally. To add insult to injury, they knocked the Hawks out of the cup too.

Pratt and Trigg had both been in excellent form and the latter finished third in the Provincial League Riders Championship. Les McGillivray had also ridden with distinction and there was much to be optimistic about. Despite a late season win at Long Eaton, Newcastle piped the Hawks to the title by 3 points – but who would have thought that possible when a team of guest riders was tracked in the opening fixtures.

1964 Provincial League Record (2/12 teams)

Played	Won	Drawn	Lost	For	Against	Pts
22	15	1	6	929	786	31

1964 Cup Record

Round 1	Home v. Exeter	Won 50-46
Round 2	Away v. Newport	Lost 40-56

1964 Provincial League Averages (captain in italics)

Rider	Mts	Rds	Pts	BP	Total	CMA
Colin Pratt	*21*	*85*	*212*	*3*	*215*	*10.12*
Roy Trigg	21	86	194	20	214	9.95
Les McGillivray	22	87	176	18	194	8.92
Len Silver	6	24	47	4	51	8.50
John Poyser	22	87	131	17	148	6.80
Brian Davies	21	70	69	14	83	4.74
Sandy McGillivray	17	63	45	10	55	3.49
Dennis Day	10	32	23	4	27	3.37

[Malcolm Brown 2.00 (3 matches only), Jimmy Heard 4.80 (5 matches only)]

1965 – A New Super League

With past squabbles forgotten, speedway took a giant leap forward with the formation of the British League. Mike Parker, whose interests spanned the country, was not interested in carrying on – particularly as Hackney had made a significant loss the previous year. Fortunately, Len Silver did not agree with him and became the sole promoter to ensure Hackney's survival. The team was mostly unchanged from the previous season, with Pratt, Trigg, Poyser, Davies and Les and Sandy McGillivray retained. Completing the team and replacing Dennis Day was Howdy Byford. Born in 1919, Byford was a former Japanese POW who was reaching the end of his career, having ridden for West Ham, Oxford, and Exeter.

The season opened with two massive away defeats – at Sheffield in a challenge match 25-50 and at Glasgow in the league by a staggering 19-59. The only redeeming feature was that Pratt missed these matches due to business commitments (or having to be talked out of retirement, depending upon which story you believe). Hackney's first home match of the season on 9 April was to produce their first ever British League win, over Sheffield 54-24. The following week's visitors, Belle Vue, were one of speedway's most famous teams, having run (uninterrupted even by war) since 1928. Hackney's 48-29 win was easier than expected.

Having lost heavily at Cradley and Swindon, Silver finally managed to secure the services of Gerald Jackson, who had refused to leave Wimbledon as directed by the rider Control Committee. Jackson was the son of former Wembley rider Jack Jackson

and, having been spotted by Aub Lawson, signed for West Ham in 1950. The following year he moved to Rayleigh, where he spent six seasons before joining Wimbledon in 1957.

Jackson made his home debut against Cradley on 23 April and did not disappoint, scoring an immaculate 12-point maximum in the Hawks' 45-32 win.

Throughout the programme there were three match races pitting former skipper Norman Hunter against three current Hawks. Hunter beat Pratt in 'The Skippers Match Race' and then beat Les McGillivray in 'The Atom Bomb Match Race' before Trigg finally got the better of the West Ham star, winning 'The Throttle Busters Match Race'.

Gerald Jackson, both reluctant and a revelation.

The unlucky John Poyser.

Colin Pratt's form was the biggest concern: having seen his CMA drop to 6 he found himself at reserve for the home match with Exeter, as in those days the team positions were determined on the average over the last six meetings. Jackson scored his second successive home maximum and the Hawks won 41½-35½. John Poyser equalled the track record in heat 5, but sadly a little over a week later his season would be over.

Heat 10 saw the first ever dead-heat recorded in the British League when Roy Trigg and Exeter's Alan Cowland were deemed inseparable behind the Falcons' Colin Gooddy.

On 7 May Hackney beat Swindon in the league at Waterden Road, 40-38. The following night the Hawks were dumped out of the Knockout Cup, losing at Edinburgh by the narrowest of margins, 46-49. Poyser crashed and broke his thigh. Further injuries followed when Hackney visited Poole on 12 May and Jackson sustained a cut eye. The eye healed but a film grew over it. (A measure of how speedway has changed is that Jackson was allowed to continue riding with a patch over the injured eye.) Hackney lost the match 30-48, but two days later beat the much-fancied West Ham at Hackney, 40-37, and completed the double at Custom House on 18 May, 42-36.

Sandy McGillivray felt that he would benefit from a move to another team and Malcolm Brown replaced him. Brown recalls:

'I bought my first bike, leathers and everything from Stan Stevens for £80. I dyed the leathers puce. I was always playing pranks and was called the clown prince. I got a second-half ride at Hackney but I broke my ankle. I took the plaster off with an axe saw blade because I wanted to ride but when I went back to the hospital, the doctor threw me out. Still, I beat Alan and Peter Jackson and was in the team. I used to entertain in the interval. I used to be in the royal signal display team, and Len wanted me to do a ramp jump. I had to ride up the steep ramp and jump through a hoop of fire. As I went up the ramp, I knocked the bike out of gear and came down the other side on the front wheel instead of the back and crushed my nuts! Len thought it was great and wanted me to do it again, but I was in agony.

'Once we were all racing at Edinburgh and Glasgow; we all went out for a few beers and then someone said, "Let's call up Len". But instead we called up Maurie Littlechild,

I put on a Scottish accent and said "Can you get in touch with Mr Silver?". We told him that Howdy Byford was caught swinging around a lamp-post without his pants drunk and disorderly and that the whole Hackney team had been arrested. In the morning we thought we had better tell him it was a joke, but when we called he had left to come up and get us out. It was lucky he had a sense of humour.'

West Ham returned on 30 July in the London Cup and their star Sverre Harrfeldt romped to an immaculate 18-point maximum, although this was not enough to stop the Hawks from beating the Hammers again, by 52-44. Harrfeldt's swoops round the boards made him a popular visitor to Waterden Road and the following week he returned to repeat the performance and win the London Riders Championship.

Hackney finished the season in eighth place and, with what was to prove their customary vice, only won twice away from home which cost them a higher place. West Ham won the inaugural British League and the London Cup, but amazingly Hackney beat the Hammers four times out of five during the season – including being the only team to complete a league double and winning the Pride of East End 44-34 at the final home meeting of the season on 15 October.

Colin Pratt had a disappointing year and his average fell by over 1½ points a match. Gerald Jackson had been the season's success story and he replaced Pratt as the number one with a string of impressive performances, particularly at home. His reward was to represent Hackney in the first British League Riders Championship (BLRC), scoring 3 points. Both Trigg and Les McGillivray's CMAs were down too – perhaps this was a measure of the increased competition faced in the new 'Super League'. Davies and Sandy McGillivray did not improve as hoped and Byford, at forty-six years of age, did as much as could be expected.

The hopes of the following season would rest on Pratt returning to his known form, potential improvement from Trigg and the emergence of promising youngster Malcolm Brown. But before that, something had to be done about the track and during the winter it was ripped up and re-laid.

1965 British League Record (8/18 teams)

Played	Won	Drawn	Lost	For	Against	Pts
34	18	1	15	1,327½	1,319½	37

1965 Cup Record

Round 1	Away v. Edinburgh	Lost 46-49

1965 British League and Cup Averages (captain in italics)

Rider	Mts	Rds	Pts	BP	Total	CMA	Maxs
Gerald Jackson	31	124	272	4	276	8.90	7
Colin Pratt	*33*	*132*	*268*	*13*	*281*	*8.52*	*7*
Roy Trigg	34	136	247½	23	270½	7.96	3
Les McGillivray	35	140	186	45	231	6.60	2
John Poyser	10	40	49	7	56	5.60	
Howdy Byford	34	136	139	34	173	5.09	
Brian Davies	33	132	122	28	150	4.55	
Malcolm Brown	19	76	60	16	76	4.00	
Sandy McGillivray	12	48	21	4	25	2.08	

1966 – Pratt's Progress

The newly banked Waterden Road circuit was unveiled to the public on 1 April and Newport had the honour of being beaten 43-35. Hackney's team was mostly unchanged from the previous year, with Pratt, Trigg, Jackson and Les McGillivray retained. Brian Davies, Malcolm Brown, Sandy McGillivray and John Poyser, returning from injury, would compete for the remaining team places. Hackney had to release one rider and Silver reluctantly went with youth over experience and Howdy Byford had to make way, moving to King's Lynn.

Although the opening match produced a victory, John Poyser had returned too early and was far from fit and Brian Davies sustained a broken shoulder.

A mixed bag of results opened the campaign, as home and away defeats against Wimbledon in challenge matches went alongside a win at King's Lynn. Ernie Baker was signed to replace Davies and he made his debut on 22 April against Belle Vue in the Hawks' opening home British League match, which was won 41-37. The opening away fixtures were lost at Swindon and Poole, whilst Exeter was beaten 43-35 at Waterden Road on 29 April.

The following week's meeting against Wolverhampton ended in controversy when Pete Jarmen walked out over track conditions. Without him his team struggled to a 46-32 defeat. Victory over King's Lynn followed on 13 May, 42-36, with the returning Byford failing to score.

Brian Davies, Willie Templeton, Colin Pratt and Maury Mattingley line up for a Hawks versus Glasgow match.

Roy Trigg made his debut at Hackney and got the key of the door on the same night.

Four days later, West Ham took 3 of the 4 points on offer over successive nights on 17 and 18 May, winning at home and drawing at the Wick. Two nights later, Hackney won at Wolverhampton 40-38 and, despite their lack of away success, found themselves second in the table, 4 points behind Coventry. It was to be short-lived, however, as rivals Wimbledon won 36-42 at Waterden Road on 3 June. This was to signal a slow but inexorable slide down the league.

Sandy McGillivray had struggled at Hackney and felt that a change of scenery would be the best for himself and the club. He was transferred, with Alan Jackson becoming a temporary replacement. John Poyser made another comeback on 17 June, but failed to score in the 48½-47½ Knockout Cup victory over Cradley. Sadly, he looked as if his confidence had gone following such a bad injury. Pratt was back to his very best, however. He finished third in the British Final, therefore qualifying for the European Final, and he also made his England debut at West Ham on 12 July, scoring 12½ points in England's 71-37 win over the Soviet Union.

Silver was certainly determined to make Hackney a success story and his efforts were rewarded when Hackney staged the first ever Great Britain versus Poland test match, held in England on 29 July. Great Britain won 61-47, with Barry Briggs unbeaten and Pratt scoring 5 wins in his 15-point haul. Antonin Woryna was best for the Poles on 10. Britain went on to win the series 3-0

Back on the domestic scene, the Hawks continued to lose away from home, suffering defeats at Newport and Cradley, followed by two successive home defeats against Halifax in the league and Wimbledon in the cup – which also saw Jackson break his hand as well as injuring his thigh and knee, ruling him out of the remainder of the season.

On 26 August Cradley were beaten 44-34 in a league match, which saw the debut of Gary Everett (who scored 2 paid 3) and, a week later, Hackney lost at home to Coventry 38-40. Pratt had a chest infection and was riding against doctor's orders. The following night it was to cost him a place in his first World Final when he was eliminated from the European Final, held at Wembley. Eight days later, Great Britain finished last with a paltry 8 points in the World Team Cup in Wroclaw. Pratt failed to score as the team's reserve rider.

The season limped to a conclusion with an embarrassing away defeat at Oxford, Roy Trigg scoring 17 of Hackney's 27 points. The London Riders Championship was again held at the Wick and former skipper Norman Hunter beat Olle Nygren in a run-off. Wimbledon won at Hackney for the fourth time that season in the London Cup, but it was West Ham that took the trophy as well as managing a draw in the annual season finale – the Pride of the East End Trophy.

Pratt had returned to his best form and, in distinguished company, he had progressed at international level too. He represented Hackney in the BLRC, scoring 2 points. Roy Trigg had also continued his improvement, but this was offset by Gerald Jackson who, hampered by injury, had not maintained his scoring from 1965. McGillivray, although slightly down pointswise, was as dependable as ever, but the season's success story was Malcolm Brown, who scored a creditable CMA of 4.46 in his first full campaign:

'Gerald Jackson and Jackie Biggs both did my bikes, but Jack was temperamental. Once I went over there and said "Hi Jack, where's my engine?". He said "It's in next door's yard". He could not balance the flywheels and so he had thrown the whole thing. Ronnie Russell was my dope and oil man. He was a rough diamond and once Ivor Brown ran me into the fence and when he came back into the fence he came over and apologised, but Ronnie rushes over, grabs him and starts to have a right go.'

The remainder of the team never really got their act together, resulting in Hackney finishing a disappointing fourteenth place in the British League table. It was obvious that the team needed another star rider and that man was to arrive with a rather large bang.

1966 British League Record (14/19 teams)

Played	Won	Drawn	Lost	For	Against	Pts
36	15	1	20	1,347½	1,456½	31

1966 Cup Record

Round 1	Bye	
Round 2	Home v. Cradley	Won 48½-47½
Round 3	Home v. Wimbledon	Lost 47-49

1966 British League and Cup Averages (captain in italics)

Rider	Mts	Rds	Pts	BP	Total	CMA	Maxs
Colin Pratt	*34*	*152*	*367*	*13*	*380*	*10.00*	*12*
Roy Trigg	38	166	340	18	358	8.63	6
Gerald Jackson	31	128	211	7	218	6.81	1
Les McGillivray	38	154	176	32	208	5.40	1
Brian Davies	9	32	36	6	42	5.25	
Malcolm Brown	38	145	147	19	166	4.58	
Ernie Baker	33	100	75	11	86	3.44	
Sandy McGillivray	13	35	20	5	25	2.86	
Gary Everett	6	17	8	4	12	2.82	
John Poyser	18	42	16	5	21	2.00	

1967 – Sizzling Banger

Further track improvements were made, with the relocating of the pits from behind the main grandstand to the end of the main straight on the fourth bend, and further team improvements were made with the allocation of former West Ham rider and Swedish international Bengt Jansson. Jansson would prove to be one of the greatest riders to ride for Hackney, and former Hawk Colin McKee, who had last ridden for the Hawks in 1963, joined him. McKee had ridden for Wolverhampton, Edinburgh and Poole in the intervening years and returned to the Wick with a 6.18 CMA. Making way for the two newcomers was the confidence-hit Poyser and, in a move unpopular with the fans, Roy Trigg joined Oxford. Roy remembers:

'I got kicked out when Banger came. I did three seasons and I was already to go again. I went to his [Silver's] office and Maurice Morley handed me a letter. I didn't open it till I got home and it said thanks for your services but you are being released and we are signing Bengt Jansson. It was a good business decision but it could have been done better. I was bitter for years.'

On the managerial side, Alec Ford, the team manager since the Hawks re-opened in 1963, left to join King's Lynn and was replaced by Maurice Morley. Completing the riding side were Pratt, Jackson, McGillivray, Brown and Davies.

The home season opened on 24 March and Glasgow managed to gain a draw in a league match. The Hawks then strung together an impressive series of home wins

against Long Eaton, West Ham, Oxford, Cradley and Edinburgh, as well as an away victory at King's Lynn, 40-38. King's Lynn's visit on 19 May produced one of the best races ever seen at Waterden road. In heat 10 Jansson trailed Norman Hunter and Terry Betts, but on the last corner the Swede swept outside Hunter, cut back inside Betts – effectively driving between the two – and sailed across the line. Hackney won 43-35.

Arguments raged at Newcastle on 12 June. Although the Hackney team stopped short of a walkout, they were so incensed by track conditions that they decided not to race competitively. Hackney lost 20-58 and former Hackney boss Mike Parker reported his old team to the SCB, who put in a counter-protest about the track conditions.

Colin McKee, a Hawk in 1963 and 1967.

Hackney 1967. From left to right: Len Silver, Colin McKee, Gary Everett, Malcolm Brown, Brian Davies, Bengt Jansson, Gerald Jackson, Les McGillivray, Colin Pratt and Maurice Morley.

The cup campaign continued and Oxford visited in round two and were beaten 53-43, despite the returning Roy Trigg scoring 12. The Hawks were pleased to complete the match with nobody injured, having lost Silver (1964), Poyser (1965) and Jackson (1966) in cup-ties in the previous three years. As in 1965, a double was completed over West Ham. The Hawks won at home 41-37 on 30 June, in which a classic heat 6 brought a heart-stopping battle between Jansson and Harrfeldt. Jansson went on to record his first British League maximum for the Hawks. The win at Custom House came four days later, 40-37.

Again controversy followed the Hawks to Cradley on 8 July. Jansson scored an immaculate 15-point maximum, despite an alarming crash after Anders Michanek drove his fellow countryman into the fence, causing Banger to ride wall-of-death style round the fence before hitting the pit gatepost. Michanek was excluded, but Hackney still lost 34-44.

The Hawks beat Wimbledon at home at the end of July, but lost Gerald Jackson with an eye injury. There was a break from the cut and thrust of league duties when Czechoslovakian team Prague visited the Wick on 4 August. Although beaten 52-26, the spectacular Czechs proved good entertainment – even if it was more down to their battles with the safety fence than their points scoring. The top scorer for the visitors with 14 points was Antonin Kasper, whose son would ride for Hackney fifteen years later. Jackson's eye injury was worse than first thought. He admitted that when sitting at the start he could not see the tapes properly. The home match against Newcastle on 18 August was his last and he retired.

Better late than never, his replacement was former World number three Jack Biggs, who had oringinally been pencilled in to ride in 1963. An Australian, Biggs had come to England in 1947 at the age of twenty-five. He rode with great distinction for Harringay and, in 1951, went down in history as the man who threw away a World Championship. Biggs won his first four rides, beating Ronnie Moore in his first and both Jack Young and Jack Parker in his second. He lined up for his last ride in heat 19 unbeaten and needing only a single point to become World Champion. He missed the gate and was forced wide on the first bend. He could not make up the ground on Aub Lawson, Split Waterman and Freddie Williams and finished last. Watermen passed Lawson on the final bend to win and set up a three-man run-off with Biggs and Jack Young. Biggs jetted into the lead in the run-off but after a lap drifted wide and gifted Young with an easy passing opportunity. Demoralised, Jack could not even hold onto second place and was passed by Waterman – his big chance had gone.

Biggs made his Hackney debut in the London Cup defeats at Wimbledon on 24 August, 33-62, and then at home against West Ham the following night. With Jansson and Harrfeldt missing, reserves were promoted into the team. Former Hawk Malcolm Simmons scored an immaculate 14-paid-15 maximum and, with Biggs scoring just 1 point, the Hammers won 42-54. After only three matches Biggs hurt his hand and missed the remainder of the season.

The cup semi-final was held at West Ham on 5 September, and the Hammers were victorious 45-51. In fact, Hackney were not happy about racing this fixture at all, since it was their fifth match in as many days, having beaten Wimbledon at home in the London Cup 50-46 on 1 September, losing at Swindon 23-55 the following night before hosting a Wolverhampton/Newport double header on 4 September, winning both matches 44-34 and 53-25.

What was to become the famous Hackney Superama meeting was held for the first time on 8 September, whilst the Hawks were being soundly beaten at Newport 22-56, and a week later Hackney fans were thrilled that both Jansson and Pratt qualified for the World Final at Wembley. Pratt scored 4 points to finish in thirteenth place, but Banger, ironically like Biggs before him, saw the title slip away in a run-off against Ove Fundin. Hackney won their remaining home league fixtures against Sheffield and Exeter and added a further away win at Wolverhampton.

The season, like the previous year, was completed with a draw against West Ham in the Pride of East End Trophy at Waterden Road on 6 October, before the Hammers beat Hackney at Custom House four days later to clinch the London Cup. The final home match of the season was held on 20 October against Wimbledon in the Metropolitan Gold Cup (MGC). Hackney won 47-31 and, as an added attraction, the enterprising Silver arranged for two special match races between Fundin and Jansson and Fundin and Pratt. In a disappointing display by the World Champion, the Hackney pair easily beat Fundin.

Hackney finished in a credible fifth position in the league, despite the perennial lack of away success. Jansson had been a revelation, winning a World Team Cup winners

London Riders Champion Colin Pratt with second-placed Malcolm Simmons.

medal with Sweden, scoring 9 points. He also represented Hackney in the BLRC and scored 8 points. Although Pratt's scoring was down by around a point a match, he made his World Final debut and rode in the team final, again failing to score from the reserve berth. He also rode for Great Britain in test matches and at West Ham in the first test against Poland he was the only rider to stand between the Poles and a massacre, scoring 13 in Great Britain's 39-69 defeat. Pratt also won the London Riders Championship, beating ex-Hawk Malcolm Simmons in a run-off. Of the rest, McKee finished as third heat leader with an average not dissimilar to his 1963 Hackney CMA. Les McGillivray and Malcolm Brown were as steady as ever, but with Gerald Jackson's CMA down by 1½ points per match, it was not difficult to see why away victories were scarce.

There was a lot to be optimistic about though, with Jansson and Pratt set to be retained and Biggs back for a full season. If that heat leader trio could find support then anything could happen.

1967 British League Record (5/19 teams)

Played	Won	Drawn	Lost	For	Against	Pts
36	20	1	15	1,402	1,400	41

1967 Cup Record

Round 1	Bye	
Round 2	Home v. Oxford	Won 53-43
Round 3	Home v. Poole	Won 53-42
Semi-final	Away v. West Ham	Lost 45-51

1967 British League and Cup Averages (captain in italics)

Rider	Mts	Rds	Pts	BP	Total	CMA	Maxs
Bengt Jansson	35	150	359	11	370	9.87	12
Colin Pratt	*39*	*168*	*362*	*14*	*376*	*8.95*	*11*
Colin McKee	39	151	209	27	236	6.25	1
Les McGillivray	39	154	185	39	224	5.82	1
Gerald Jackson	26	90	108	12	120	5.33	
Malcolm Brown	39	141	158	20	178	5.05	1
Gary Everett	13	33	33	8	41	4.97	
Brian Davies	37	127	120	28	148	4.66	

[Jack Biggs 6.33 (3 matches only)]

Superama

Superama was unique in speedway. It was conceived so that Hackney could host a fixture at Waterden Road whilst the Hackney team rode at a fellow Friday night team.

This meant that no home rider was ever in the line-up, making it a truly open individual event. The field assembled was always superb and would have graced any World Final line-up. Over the years many Superamas produced unexpected thrills and controversy.

The first Superama was held in 1967 whilst the Hawks were away at Newport. Speedway legends Barry Briggs, Ivan Mauger, Gote Nordin and Olle Nygren were in the opening meeting, which started in fine style when Bob Kilby broke the track record in the first heat, setting a new time of 66.0. However, at the end of the night it was Barry Briggs who had scorched to victory with a fifteen point maximum.

There always seemed to be one unlucky rider in Superama. In 1969, the meeting was not decided until a heat 19 showdown between Briggs and Mauger, who were both unbeaten on 12 points. Mauger led from the start and had established a comfortable lead when disaster struck. His bike developed problems which caused him to fall, handing Briggs a gift victory for his second Superama success. The following year Soren Sjostens finished the 1970 Superama unbeaten on track having defeated Ivan Mauger and the eventual winner Ronnie Moore. But a tape exclusion in his second ride cost him dearly.

In 1971 Briggs was unbeaten on track, but a third ride engine failure cost him victory and bizarrely Christer Lofqvist scored an unbeaten 12 in 1972, but an exclusion under the two minute rule cost him victory after he inexplicably went missing between heats.

Having commenced life as programme filler, Superama became a speedway classic whose roll of honour reads like who's who of international speedway. Six different World Champions won Superama but like that other London classic, the London Riders Championship, no rider ever managed to win it three times.

Superama Roll of Honour

1967	Barry Briggs
1968	Anders Michanek
1969	Barry Briggs
1970	Ronnie Moore
1971	Ray Wilson
1972	Ivan Mauger
1973	Anders Michanek
1974	John Louis
1975	Martin Ashby
1976	Dave Jessup
1977	Malcolm Simmons
1978	Peter Collins
1979	Ole Olsen
1980	Dave Jessup
1981	Phil Crump

1968 – So Near And Yet ...

The seeds of success that had been so carefully sown began to pay dividends and the Hawks won their first eight league matches to head the British League. Wolverhampton, Glasgow, King's Lynn, Swindon, Wimbledon, Oxford and Leicester were beaten at Waterden Road, with an away win at King's Lynn on 4 May, 42-36, thrown in for good measure. Lining up for the Hawks were Pratt, Jansson, McGillivray, Biggs, and Brown. Colin McKee returned to New Zealand and Brian Davies was transferred to King's Lynn. Completing the team were Gary Everett and Des Lukehurst, who had been signed from Oxford. An unknown young New Zealander called Graeme Smith was signed and loaned to Hackney's new sister track Rayleigh (which Silver had re-opened to join the new British League Division Two). Joining him on loan there was Laurie Etheridge. On the managerial side, Maurice Morley had resigned as team manager and was replaced by Dave Erskine.

Malcolm Brown and Len Silver in discussion.

Jack Biggs and Colin Pratt in a 5-1 position over Coatbridge, leading Bert Harkins and Reidar Eide.

Amongst this great start, Hackney exited the cup at the first hurdle at West Ham on 16 April, 52-55, before slipping to the first league defeat of the season at Exeter on 13 May, 21-57. Hackney visited newly re-opened Leicester on 21 May. With Jansson and Michanek missing, a battle royal developed and going into the last heat the scores were locked together 36-36. It looked grim for Hackney, tracking Lukehurst who had scored 2 and Brown who had failed to score against Leicester heat leaders Ray Wilson and John Boulger. The race that developed was a classic, with passing and re-passing and never more than a bike's length between the four riders. Amazingly, Lukehurst and Brown managed to keep Boulger behind them and, against the odds, Hackney forced a draw. Pratt and Biggs had previously kept Hackney in the meeting, scoring 11 and 10 points respectively.

Another draw was gained at Poole on 5 June and Cradley were dispatched at Waterden Road two days later 43-35, with Trigg scoring 12 for Cradley. The Hawks then lost at London rivals West Ham and Wimbledon, which made another away win an urgent priority. A tough match was expected at title challengers Coventry on 22 June, but the win slipped away – the situation not being helped when Pratt broke the tapes in heat 9. Hackney lost 36-41.

A break from league racing came on 12 July when Hackney hosted the World League match between Great Britain and Poland. The Poles were annihilated 60-18, with Pratt scoring an 11-paid-12 maximum. England went on to easily win the World League. Whilst the test was being fought at Waterden Road, the Hawks were being beaten at Newport 32-46. There was controversy at Sheffield on 25 July when Bengt Larsson speared Jack Biggs. Back in the pits, Biggs hit Larsson with a right hook. The Sheffield promoter, the legendary Red Devil Frank Varey, decided to get involved and floored Biggs. Silver then waded in to help Biggs and Varey floored him too! The match, overshadowed as it was by bad tempers and fighting, finished as a 35-43 defeat.

As August commenced, Hackney were still top of the table, 2 points clear of West Ham with Coventry in third place. A mini Scottish tour followed over successive nights on 2 and 3 August. A second away win was gained at Glasgow 42-36, but Coatbridge was victorious twenty-four hours later 25-53. Prague returned on 9 August for the second season running and fared better, losing 46-32. Kasper was again the top scorer; now with Coventry, he scored 10. Kasper was back on 30 August, scoring 4 paid 5 as the Hawks critically beat rivals Coventry 42-36.

Pratt retained the London Riders Championship and Hackney also hosted the first Second Division Riders Championship. Representing Rayleigh, Hackney's Graeme Smith finished third with 11 points.

Olle Nygren leading Jack Biggs at Wimbledon.

The season's finale was going to be hard and, critically, with Jansson missing again, Hackney lost at Wolverhampton 38-40, despite Etheridge scoring 8 points. Biggs was injured and was joined the next night by Lukehurst as Hackney lost at Halifax 24-54.

The Hawks raced three important league matches on successive days. They lost at Oxford 33-45 before winning their final home match against Newport on 4 October 48-30. The following night the Hawks lost 32-46 at Cradley and, with Coventry winning at King's Lynn, the league was completed with both Hackney and Coventry inseparable on 44 points. Sadly, Coventry had superior race points and were crowned as League Champions. It was a bitter pill to swallow having come so close to the title. Silver blamed the Swedish authorities for the amount of matches Jansson missed (5) for the loss of the championship.

The season finished with modern-day stars dropping their handlebars and leg-trailing in a tribute to pre-war stars as the Hackney Wolves took on Lea Bridge in a special challenge match that finished 14-39. The Hawks had enjoyed a great season, despite narrowly losing out on honours – including the London Cup where, despite Hackney's strength, Wimbledon emerged victorious.

Pratt and Jansson swapped places for the top spot and both scored well, despite neither qualifying for the World Final. Pratt retained the London Riders Championship and represented the team in the BLRC and scored 2 points. There was no real third heat leader but with McGillivray, Lukehurst, Brown and Biggs all scoring solidly, Hackney had strength in depth. The question was could Hackney go one better?

1968 British League Record (2/19 teams)

Played	Won	Drawn	Lost	For	Against	Pts
36	21	2	13	1,421	1,383	44

1968 Cup Record

Round 1	Away v. West Ham	Lost 52-55

1968 British League and Cup Averages (captain in italics)

Rider	Mts	Rds	Pts	BP	Total	CMA	Maxs
Colin Pratt	*36*	*152*	*350*	*14*	*364*	*9.58*	*5*
Bengt Jansson	32	137	291	17	308	8.99	5
Les McGillivray	37	146	203	43	246	6.74	
Des Lukehurst	34	127	175	23	198	6.24	
Jack Biggs	33	127	169	24	193	6.08	
Malcolm Brown	37	134	158	20	178	5.31	1
Alan Jackson	8	20	19	3	22	4.40	
Gary Everett	33	99	90	11	101	4.08	
Laurie Etheridge	8	24	13	6	19	3.17	

1969 – Cass Turns On The Gas

'Oh how the mighty have fallen' may sum up 1969. The rider control committee had taken Jansson, although in the event he did not ride in England. Everett had joined Wimbledon and Brown moved on to the scene of his triumphant last-heat ride the previous season and joined Leicester. Replacing them was Tommy Sweetman, who had won the first ever post-war race at the Wick in 1963, signed from Exeter. Graeme Smith was recalled from Rayleigh and Jimmy Gooch was signed from Newport. Born on 16 November 1928, Gooch was coming to the end of his career, having ridden with great distinction for Wembley, Swindon, New Cross, Bradford, Ipswich and Norwich. He had been sacked from Norwich after an incident with Ove Fundin. He remembers the fracas well:

'I was leading Fundin but he came from behind and ran me over. When I got back to the pits I was so mad, I clumped him. I went into his special place and clouted him and they sacked me on the spot, but Danny Dunton was there from Oxford and he hired me. Sacked and hired in two seconds.'

At Oxford in 1965 he had his best year, finishing fourteenth in his only World Final appearance with 3 points, representing Great Britain in the World Team Cup (scoring 3 from the reserve berth) and finishing with a 10.59 CMA. Pratt, McGillivray, Biggs and Lukehurst were retained to complete the team, but from the outset the problem was obvious: many of the line-up were past their peak.

The opening home match was staged on 21 March and Glasgow were beaten 39-38 in the league. King's Lynn won the Anglian trophy and the MGC was completed against Wimbledon and West Ham, which predictably produced home wins and away defeats. It was not until 18 April that Hackney rode another home British League match, losing against Belle Vue 32-46, preceding another home loss against Newcastle and defeats at Belle Vue and Poole.

Sweetman seemed completely lost at Waterden Road and he was transferred to his former club Wolverhampton. Replacing him was Australian Garry Middleton, who made his debut on 9 May, scoring 5 in the 44-34 win league win over Coatbridge. Middleton was born in Corowa, New South Wales on 19 July 1948. 'A character' is an understated way to describe the rider who was dubbed 'Cass the Gas'. He first rode in Adelaide in 1966 and came to England to ride for Belle Vue in 1967, scoring a 2.60 CMA from six matches.

That season he also rode for King's Lynn before settling at Wimbledon. He stayed with the Dons for 1968 and improved his average to 5.87 before joining the Newcastle in the early part of 1969 before his move back to London. Middleton's gutsy performances ensured the team at least showed some fight.

July started well as rivals Wimbledon were beaten at the Wick on 4 July. Middleton scored a 12-point maximum, but his scoring was inconsistent and, with Gooch and Lukehurst both injured (a cracked shoulder and knee ligament trouble respectively), Hackney continued to struggle. When Lukehurst was fit again he found himself transferred to Romford and was replaced by Brian Leonard. Leonard was born on 19 February 1946 and had started riding second halves at Oxford in 1962. He had spent

Coatbridge leads Jimmy Gooch and Garry Middleton.

the last four seasons at West Ham, scoring over 7 points a match for the Hammers in 1967. Fellow struggler Smith was sent back to Rayleigh with Laurie Etheridge coming the other way to ride for the Hawks full-time. Etheridge was born on 12 September 1944 and had started riding at the Weymouth training school in the winter of 1966/67 before joining Exeter. Gooch returned from injury on 8 August but did not score and Wimbledon beat Hackney in the London Cup 30-47.

The following night Hackney visited Cradley and for the second time the police had to be called to quell crowd trouble. Roy Trigg recalls:

'He [Middleton] came under me at about a million miles an hour. I saw him coming so I knocked off early and he sailed past me and went straight into the fence. He went back into the pits and then came back with a gun in his hand. I never took it seriously and started laughing. I don't know what it was, I thought it was a water pistol. They had to drag him out of the pits and get him out of there, the Cradley crowd were after him.'

Middleton broke his wrist but insisted on carrying on. Pratt also took a stretcher ride and to complete the misery the Hawks were beaten 28-49.

Coventry were beaten at Waterden Road on 15 August 41-37 before a welcome respite from league action. The following week former Hawk Trevor Hedge won the Londons Riders Championship and, on 29 August, Hackney again had the privilege of staging a test match, this time England versus New Zealand.

England won the deciding third test 68-40, with Pratt contributing 8 points. Briggs and Mauger provided the only resistance, scoring 16 and 14 respectively.

September provided the last opportunity to climb the league. It proved to be a disaster. There were away defeats at Halifax, Coventry, Glasgow and Coatbridge. The three home matches provided just one win, against Sheffield, as both Swindon and King's Lynn won at Hackney. In fact the only good news during this period was Silver's programme notes for the 37-41 defeat by King's Lynn on 19 September – when he promised the fans that Jansson would return for the following season.

The Hawks completed the league campaign on 3 October by beating Newport 47-30. However, that was not enough to avoid the wooden spoon position, Hackney finishing in nineteenth place, 3 points behind West Ham. Hackney had failed to win any away matches and on 10 occasions the home team amassed over 50 points. They lost six times at home and only managed a draw on another two occasions. Hackney's descent from second to last place in successive seasons was the largest fall from grace recorded. A measure of the disastrous year was that Hackney's top scorer Pratt saw his CMA fall to 7.35 – over 2 points a match down on the previous year – and no Hackney rider qualified for the BLRC. Middleton had done well and recorded his highest CMA to date as well as adding some much needed colour to the team. The team was solid thereafter, but no one emerged to back the top two.

Wimbledon clinched the London Cup as the season limped to a disappointing end before the final meeting of the season saw Hackney beat West Ham in the annual Pride of the East End Trophy, 45-33. Jansson had been missed and everyone prayed for his return. Silver's programme notes for the West Ham match contained news unlikely to provide the Hackney fans with much comfort in the short term, but would in time prove to be the most significant rider story ever reported: 'Two riders with obvious big futures ahead of them in whom I am more than passing interested. I have already bid for the services of both of them and there inclusion in our final meeting is therefore no accident. Their names? Geoff Ambrose and Barry Thomas, Barry is one the brightest seventeen year olds I have ever seen.'

Graeme Smith – dropped and then swapped.

1969 British League Record, 19/19

Played	Won	Drawn	Lost	For	Against	Pts
36	10	2	24	1,229	1,573	22

1969 Cup Record

Round 1	Away v. Coatbridge	Lost 25-53

1969 British League and Cup Averages (captain in italics)

Rider	Mts	Rds	Pts	BP	Total	CMA	Maxs
Colin Pratt	*36*	*147*	*255*	*15*	*270*	*7.35*	*3*
Garry Middleton	28	118	199	9	208	7.05	1
Jack Biggs	37	144	206	22	228	6.33	
Jimmy Gooch	31	120	165	20	185	6.17	
Les McGillivray	37	135	155	29	184	5.45	1
Laurie Etheridge	19	73	74	19	93	5.10	
Brian Leonard	19	66	71	12	83	5.03	
Des Lukehurst	18	59	64	8	72	4.88	
Tommy Sweetman	7	24	23	4	27	4.50	
Graeme Smith	25	71	41	14	55	3.10	

HACKNEY HERO
COLIN PRATT

Survivor of GE.57.86

Colin Pratt was born in Hoddesdon, Hertfordshire on 10 October 1938. He first rode for Southampton, making his debut on 7 June 1960 against Oxford. The following year he commenced the season riding for Poole, but after just two matches he was transferred to Stoke, where he spent the next three seasons.

'I was at Stoke when they were at Sun Street. They closed and I asked to go to Sheffield, but they wouldn't let me go and so I went to Swindon in the National League. After a month I signed for Hackney under the promotion of Mike Parker. When Parker left, Len [Silver] asked me to stay on and ride for Hackney and I stayed there for six years.' But wasn't there a big worry about riding under the black? 'There were plenty of matches in the Provincial League, but if it had carried on the big risk was that you lost your World Championship rounds. But at the end of the season they had a match Sheffield versus Belle Vue to bring everyone to their senses and that led to the formation of the British League in '65. I just took a risk it would not go on and on.'

Colin became skipper of the Hawks and formed a formidable partnership with Bengt Jansson. 'Me and Banger was there for a few years as the top two, we swapped top spot a couple of times but then the Swedes were banned and we signed Garry Middleton. He was wild man, you never knew what he was going to do next. Jackie Biggs tuned my engines for the whole ten years I was in speedway. He used to treat me like a son.

'The big highlight there was winning the London Riders Championship two years on the trot. Nobody ever won it three times. The third year I won my first two races then dropped a chain in my third ride that cost me three in a row. It was the oldest trophy in history and I wanted to do it.'

Colin became a full England international, riding in two World Team Cup finals and qualified for the 1967 World Final.

'The year before I got through to the European Final but I had pleurisy and the night before I was in bed and I rode but got knocked out. The next year I qualified it was the highlight of my career. We had a great team spirit and Lenny was a great promoter. I had a good relationship with him, even though I left in the end. I just fancied a change, but I enjoyed my Hackney days.'

Colin's career was tragically cut short in the Lokeren Road disaster, but went on to become a successful promoter and team manager at Rye House, King's Lynn and Cradley before returning to London in 1996.

Having successfully ridden the old Hackney track and been part of the consortium that brought speedway back in 1996, what is Colin's view of both circuits?

'The old track was very good, brilliant – especially the shape, you could ride in and out. Barry Briggs used to say that it was too fast for a small track. The banking built up over the years and eventually they brought it in to avoid the lamp standards. When we opened in '96 it was such a shame that it never worked out, especially since we had such a successful Grand Prix. Years ago, families used to walk right across Hackney marshes to get to the track and they don't do it now. It was a new track but the stadium was built for greyhounds and the viewing was not as good as the old Hackney. But, basically, the area had changed.'

Colin is still involved in speedway today at Coventry.

Pratty works on his bike in the old Hackney pits.

3

THE WICK FLICKERS
1970-79

1970 – The 'Atom Bomb' Goes Off

Jansson did return, but Pratt at last carried out his threat and moved on to Cradley. Replacing him, coming in the reverse direction, was Bob Andrews. Born on 27 October 1935 in Edmonton, London, Andrews had first ridden for Wimbledon and stayed with the Dons for nine successive seasons until he joined Wolverhampton in the new British League in 1965. During these years he rode in four World Finals, riding as reserve in the 1960 final before finishing in an impressive fifth position at Malmo in 1961 with 10 points, and joint fifth the following year at Wembley, scoring 9. His final appearance came in 1964 when he finished in twelfth place with 4 points. During this time, Andrews emigrated and became a New Zealand citizen. He did not return for the 1966 and '67 seasons, but returned to England and joined Cradley for the 1968 and '69 season, where he became World Pairs Champions in 1969, scoring 10 paid 15 for New Zealand to add to Ivan Mauger's 18. Brian Leonard returned to West Ham and Graeme Smith was swapped for Barry Thomas, who would remain on loan to Canterbury, doubling up as required. The remainder of the team comprised of the retained Middleton, Biggs, Gooch, Etheridge and the new captain, McGillivray.

The season got underway at Wimbledon on 19 March with a heavy defeat in the MGC. Twenty-four hours later the home season opened against Newport in the British League. Middleton had not recovered from the previous season's wrist injury and would miss the opening meetings, which gave Thomas an early debut scoring 3 paid 4 in the 47-31 victory. Hackney staged an early test match, this time against Australia on 17 April. The match was rained off after nine heats with the score 30-24 and was never re-staged.

For the third year running, Hackney failed to get past the first round of the cup, losing 34-44 at Wimbledon on 23 April. On 29 May, West Ham won 38-40 at the Wick and the following night Hackney were the first opponents to ride at Wembley's famous Empire stadium since 1956. 20,000 people watched an exciting battle before the Hawks succumbed 37-41. A fortnight later, on 12 June, Wembley rode at the Wick for the first time since the war, Hackney winning 52-26. Ex-Hawk Des Lukehurst failed to score and former World Champion Ove Fundin scored a disappointing 3 paid 4 points. Hackney took on Cradley on 26 June, which saw the return of Colin Pratt. He failed to score and the Hawks won 48-30 with another former Hawk, Roy Trigg, scoring 11. It was to be

Bob Andrews.

Colin Pratt's last appearance at the track he had graced for so many seasons. Less than three weeks later Pratt's racing career would be over.

West Ham visited the Wick in the London Cup on 10 July and were beaten 56-22. Four days later half their team would be dead. Returning from a challenge match in Holland, the mini-bus they were travelling in crashed with two lorries – both carrying tree trunks – and a petrol tanker. Such was the impact that the vehicles would go on to crash into a house. Four riders, including ex-Hawk Gary Everett, were killed, as was legendary pre-war racer and West Ham team manager Phil Bishop. Pratt was guesting for the Hammers and he sustained a broken neck as well as fracturing a kneecap. He would never ride competitively again. The incident, known as the Lokeren Road disaster, was the worse loss speedway had ever suffered. Andrews recalls what life was like back in the UK waiting for news:

'I shared a workshop with Colin Pratt and Peter Bradshaw, at Pratty's mother-in-law's place in Harlow. I was there when the accident in Holland happened. I manned the phones at Pratty's place, and played with the kids (young Troy was a handful). I was very annoyed when Charles Ochilltree, who was running West Ham, rang in and asked me to remind Shirley Bradshaw that Peter, who had died, still owed a couple of hundred pounds for the bike he had…'

Hackney's season was again ruined by injuries. Banger broke bones in his hand whilst riding for Sweden in a test match at West Ham. This injury would cost him a World Final place, as he could not ride in the European Final. However, a worse fate awaited Biggs. During a meaningless second-half event at Wembley, he broke his pelvis and never rode in England again. Biggs had always planned for 1970 to be his last season in England, but to have his career in this country finish in such a way was disappointing. Without these two, Hackney lost at home to Poole and also at Newport, Cradley and Halifax and Swindon. Middleton was in the middle of a real purple patch, scoring 17 at Swindon and only being denied the London Riders Championship after an oiled-up plug stopped him from leaving the starting gate in his fourth ride. He won his other races, but it was not enough to stop Trevor Hedge retaining his title. Jansson returned on the 21 August, but could only score 1 point and Hackney lost 37-41 to Wimbledon in the London Cup. In the same competition, Hackney won at West Ham 45-33 on 25 August and also beat Wembley at Waterden Road 44-34 in the London Cup North on 4 September. The return at Wembley would be run as a second half, as Wembley had a lack of home fixtures available. Wimbledon went on to win the competition.

Jack Biggs leads the falling Reidar Eide and Bengt Jansson.

Hackney, 1970. From left to right, back row: Len Silver, Les McGillivray, Bengt Jansson, Garry Middleton, Laurie Etheridge, Dave Erskine. Front row: Jack Biggs, Jimmy Gooch, Bob Andrews.

Hackney beat Belle Vue 44-34 at Hackney on 11 September. The next night Hackney lost at Coventry 33-44 in the British League and lost Andrews with a broken wrist. He returned to New Zealand and never rode for Hackney again. Rayleigh was becoming an effective nursery for the Hawks, with several riders looking like they may make the grade for Hackney. Allen Emmett, Hugh Saunders and Geoff Maloney would be used as cover for Andrews. Hackney gained their solitary away success of the year by winning at Wolverhampton, which left them in eleventh place in the final league table. The season was completed with a 49-29 win over the tragedy-stricken West Ham in the traditional Pride of the East End Trophy.

Jansson finished the year injured again after a crash in Sweden, but his return had yielded his normal high scores and had provided Hackney with a proper number one, and he was ably backed by Middleton – who improved his CMA by over a point a match. Etheridge had not scored as many as expected and Andrews never really settled at

Veterans Jimmy Gooch and Les McGillivray.

1970 programme.

HACKNEY SPEEDWAY

Meeting No. 24
8th Season

HACKNEY v SWINDON
(British League Division One)

FRIDAY AUGUST 28th 1970 at 8.00

Betting Strictly Prohibited

Official Magazine Programme - 2/-

Waterden Road. 'I didn't want to go to Hackney; I enjoyed Cradley, but they wanted Pratty more than they wanted me. So I asked for a lot to go there, and I got it, it must have been Cradley that paid. I got a new Jawa, but I was really a JAP rider, but Uncle Len said JAWA was the way to go, and he even got the supporters to buy us all a battery ignition that the Swedes used, and that made the bike spin even more, and I was pretty good at throttle control (on a JAP) but you had to ride JAWAs full throttle, so I was on one bike for some meetings and the other one at other meetings. I was doing myself no favours.'

Biggs had been unlucky and fellow veterans Gooch and McGillivray had both decided to retire, McGillivray having set an all-time British League record for consecutive appearances. Starting in Hawks' first British League match at Glasgow on 2 April 1965, he never missed an official match until his last league performance against Leicester 223 matches later. With the veterans all making their last appearances for Hackney, a new line-up would be assembled for the new season. Having ridden in 14 matches, scoring a CMA of 3.59 and having had a successful year at Canterbury – which included winning the Junior Championship of the British Isles – Barry Thomas would be one of the replacements.

1970 British League Record (11/19 teams)

Played	Won	Drawn	Lost	For	Against	Pts
36	15	2	19	1,369½	1,435½	32

1970 Cup Record

Round 1	Away v. Wimbledon	Lost 34-44

1970 British League and Cup Averages (captain in italics)

Rider	Mts	Rds	Pts	BP	Total	CMA	Maxs
Bengt Jansson	26	117	268½	9	277½	9.49	7
Garry Middleton	35	160	317	11	328	8.20	2
Jack Biggs	19	77	103	14	117	6.08	
Bob Andrews	33	137	171	35	206	6.02	
Jimmy Gooch	37	135	177	24	201	5.96	1
Laurie Etheridge	35	120	121	24	145	4.83	
Les McGillivray	*37*	*124*	*116*	*30*	*146*	*4.71*	
Barry Thomas	14	49	37	7	44	3.59	

1971 – The Magnificent Seven

Andrews returned to Cradley, leaving four new riders to be found. Gary Middleton was appointed the new Hackney skipper, joining Jansson, Etheridge and Thomas. Czech Miroslav Verner, described in the opening night's programme as 'Dark, handsome and a fireball' was allocated to the team and also joining was Eddie Reeves. Reeves was born on 8 April 1946 in Highgate, London and, prior to turning to speedway, he had a trial for West Ham United Football Club. He made his speedway debut for New Cross in 1963, where he partnered his father, Reg, and had ridden in the very first post-war race at Waterden Road in 1963. Hackney scored a 5-0 in that race after Reg had engine failure and Eddie fell. He had ridden for Oxford for the last seven seasons and came to Hackney with a 5.89 CMA. Laurie Guilfoyle was given a chance in the final spot, but waiting in the wings were Rayleigh loanees Allen Emmett, Hugh Saunders and Geoff Maloney.

The opening match of the season was at home to Wolverhampton on 19 March in the British League. On his full-time debut Thomas scored a brilliant 11 points, but that did not prevent a 36-42 defeat. Hackney opened their away campaign at Reading three days later, winning the MGC match 43-35, but Reeves sustained a broken ankle. He recalls the incident: 'I was having a quite a good race with Jeff Curtis and we came out of the corner and locked up together and crashed. I broke my fibia and tibia – it's part of the job.'

2 April saw Cradley lose at Hackney 48-30. There was no sign of Verner and Silver issued a 'get here within ten days or stay away for good' ultimatum. Defeat at Exeter and at home to Reading preceded a 40-38 league win at Poole. Verner chose the stay-away-for-good option and never rode for Hackney. Attempts were made to sign Sverre Hardfeldt, who had struggled on return from serious injury, but in the end Hackney were allocated unknown Dane Preben Rosenkilde. Rosenkilde failed to score on his debut at Wimbledon in the MGC on 29 April. The Hawks were 6 points down after heat 8 and introduced both Middleton and Jansson as double tactical substitutes in heat 9. The pair raced to a 5-1, which was repeated in the following heat after Thomas passed former World Champion Ronnie Moore. Heat 11 was shared and was followed by another classic encounter that saw Moore and Jansson passing and re-passing each other before the Swede clinched it. The Hawks led 38-34 going into the final race, where another Middleton/Jansson 5-1 wrapped up the match 43-35.

Thomas was in glorious form and Silver commented in his programme notes against Exeter on 7 May, begging the question 'Can anybody doubt he is destined to be one of the all time greats?' Hackney scrapped a win 40-38, but lost Thommo with a cracked shoulder. Despite this setback, the Hawks beat West Ham 45-33 at Waterden Road the following week to clinch the MGC trophy. Guilfoyle was struggling and he went to Canterbury in a swap for Graham Miles and Dave Kennett was signed on loan from Eastbourne. Another away win at the expense of West Ham, 46-32, followed, but sadly that was wiped out when Wembley won at the Wick on 28 May 38-40. Reeves returned in this match and Miles made his debut, scoring 1 point. Rosenkilde was struggling badly, and he was released to join West Ham. Maloney, Kennett and Saunders were used to replace him. Having recovered from the injuries sustained at Lokeren, Colin Pratt asked

Garry Middleton with the Golden Helmet.

to resurrect his career, but difficulties over his insurance settlement would ensure that he never made a comeback – although Silver would try to tempt him again in 1973.

On 5 June, the Hawks pulled off a 42-36 win at Swindon in the cup – ensuring Hackney progressed past the first stage for the first time since 1967. West Ham visited again on 25 June. It was a sad time for the Hammers, who had never really recovered from the previous year's tragedy and, with doubts surrounding their future, it was hardly surprising that the team were at the bottom of the league. Hackney won 56-22, with Rosenkilde failing to score for the Hammers.

The following week, the reigning World Champion Ivan Mauger was in town with Belle Vue. He was already a legend, having become the first rider win three successive World Championships. Neither Middleton nor Thomas were the type to respect this fact though and, in beating Mauger, Middleton broke the track record.

As for Thomas, he and Mauger had an almighty scrap with each passing and re-passing each other until Mauger clinched it on the line. It was not the last time the two would battle it out in a classic Waterden Road race. Belle Vue won 36-42. Sheffield and King's Lynn visited on 16 July for a double header. The Hawks won the first match 46-32, but bad news awaited, as Miles recounts:

'I was taken off in my first race against Sheffield by Reg Wilson after he reared at the gate and took us both through the fence. I broke four bones in my foot. But Eddie Reeves had been injured earlier on and I carried on.

'In heat 7 of the second match I was trying to break up the King's Lynn team riding and on the third lap I had a big lick around the fence and almost got round Malcolm [Simmons] but I clipped the wire, got dragged through the fence and broke my back in five places. It was all my own doing, but I have no regrets.'

Hackney won 39-38, but the victory came at a terrible cost as Miles was confined to a wheelchair for the rest of his life.

The cup campaign continued at King's Lynn on 31 July. A classic encounter finished with a draw, which would require a replay at the Wick, but the up-and-down season continued. Hackney lost at home to Leicester, drew at Cradley, won at home against

Poole, lost at Wembley and drew away again, this time at Reading. Another double-header on 3 September saw Newport beaten in the league 46-32 and then the Hawks moved into the cup semi-finals, winning the replay against King's Lynn 49-29. Wimbledon were beaten in the London Cup on 10 September, 53-25, and a week later Hackney moved into a major cup final for the first time since before the war by beating Halifax at the Wick 50-27.

Unlike the previous rounds, the final would be held over two legs. The first leg was held at Cradley on 4 October. Jansson led the way for Hackney, scoring 10, and he was ably backed by Thomas (8) and Middleton (7). Hackney finally went down 37-41, but the hero of the hour was Hugh Saunders, who scored an invaluable 8 points. Saunders was born on 25 November 1944 at Vazon Bay, Guernsey. He was signed from Eastbourne in 1970 and immediately loaned to Rayleigh. The return leg was staged at Waterden Road four days later. It was a non-event. Hackney romped home, thrashing Cradley 51-27 with Jansson scoring a 12-point maximum and Thomas paid for the lot. Former Hawks Andrews and Trigg scored 5 and 3. As with the away leg, a second-string rider rose to the occasion. This time it was Dave Kennett, who scored 9 points paid 11. Kennett was born the eldest of three speedway-racing brothers on 18 April 1952 in Farnborough, Kent and there were high hopes that he would go all the way to the top.

Hackney made their last ever appearance at Custom House on 12 October, beating West Ham 42-36 in the London Cup. Hackney had won all six matches against the Hammers in their final season. Two nights later and Hackney won at Wimbledon to

Dave Kennett.

clinch the London Cup for the first time since 1936, also winning all six matches against the Dons. Hackney finished in seventh place in the final league table and, with three trophies in the cabinet, it was the best season since Hackney reopened. Jansson had enjoyed his best ever season, winning the London Riders Championship and finishing third in the World Final, although he disappointingly only scoring 1 in the BLRC. Middleton was a surprisingly inspirational captain and Thomas had been a sensation in his first full season, which saw him make his debut for England against Sweden in the second test match at Wimbledon on 22 July, scoring 4 points in England's 51-57 defeat. He was well on his way to the stardom predicted for him. The team's tail was still too long though: Etheridge slightly improved, but not to the level expected, whilst Saunders, Kennett and fellow loanee Geoff Maloney all scored around the 4-point mark. Eddie Reeves struggled with the broken ankle and the injury to Miles overshadowed everything.

Considering Verner never arrived and his replacement, Rosenkilde, never settled, Hackney rode well and now, with a young team with much potential, the fans could look forward to a rosy future. Sadly, more injuries and more missing foreigners would take its toll.

1971 British League Record (7/19 teams)

Played	Won	Drawn	Lost	For	Against	Pts
36	17	4	15	1,410	1,393	38

1971 Cup Record

Round 1	Bye	
Round 2	Away v. Swindon	Won 42-36
Round 3	Away v. King's Lynn	Draw 39-39
Round 3	Home v. King's Lynn	Won 49-29 (replay)
Semi-final	Home v. Halifax	Won 50-27
Final	H & A v. Cradley	Won 88-68 (aggregate)

1971 British League and Cup Averages (captain in italics)

Rider	Mts	Rds	Pts	BP	Total	CMA	Maxs
Bengt Jansson	36	159	393	15	408	10.26	10
Garry Middleton	*42*	*181*	*398*	*8*	*406*	*8.97*	*6*
Barry Thomas	40	172	279	34	313	7.28	3
Laurie Etheridge	42	169	192	38	230	5.44	
Hugh Saunders	23	73	79	10	89	4.87	
Eddie Reeves	30	99	97	22	119	4.81	
Dave Kennett	18	55	54	10	64	4.66	
Geoff Maloney	16	49	45	10	55	4.49	
Graham Miles	13	45	44	5	49	4.36	
Preben Rosenkilde	7	24	20	4	24	4.00	

1972 – Middle Gone

The praise Silver extended to skipper Middleton did not extend to lavish financial rewards. During the winter, Middleton wanted to stay in the UK and Silver agreed that he could run the Hackney training school. During this time the following year's contract was discussed and Middleton demanded a large increase. Silver declined and Cass moved on to Oxford. New Zealander Roger Wright replaced him. Retained from the previous year was the new captain Jansson, Thomas, Reeves, Etheridge and, making permanent moves to Waterden Road, Dave Kennett and Hugh Saunders.

The season commenced with a home match against King's Lynn in the Gold Cup. Perhaps not surprisingly, the Hawks lost 32-46 with the obvious problem being no star replacement for Middleton. Despite this, Hackney won at Reading 40-38 on 20 March and in the following home match beat Newport to get the league season underway, winning 40-38. Mixed fortunes continued as the Hawks lost the return at King's Lynn, but they did do the double home and away on Good Friday over West Ham's replacements, Ipswich. Little did they know that the Witches would become Hackney's bogey team in more ways than one. 5 May brought Ipswich's second visit and perhaps the seeds of future rivalry were sown in Silver's programme notes when he questioned the use of a guest rider for Tommy Johansson, who was in the Swedish Army: 'I am in the process of investigating the circumstances under which Ipswich are allowed a guest and if there is anything even slightly contrary to our very complicated regulations, I shall object in the strongest possible way.' In the end, Hackney were victorious 41-37, with Geoff Maloney scoring 9 paid 10. As a result of this form, Maloney moved up to being a full- time rider, replacing the out-of-touch Wright, who joined Middlesbrough in Division Two. Born on 24 July 1945, Maloney had been nicknamed 'Captain Scarlet' by Silver's daughter, due to his resemblance to the 1960s TV character. He had spent the last four seasons at Rayleigh and was currently scoring in excess of 10 points a match.

10 June saw Hackney start their defence of the Knockout Cup – against the team they defeated in the previous year's final, Cradley. Sadly, they were drawn away but a huge effort secured the Hawks a draw and a home replay. The replay with Cradley was held on 26 June, and Hackney stormed home 52-26, inspired by an outstanding 12-point maximum by Thomas. Former Hawk Bob Andrews valiantly tried to stem the tide for Cradley, scoring 10 points and inflicting Jansson's only defeat in heat 12.

A break from league action took place on 14 July when Australia took on Sweden in the Inter Nations Championship. The match had been scheduled for the previous week, but had been rained off. The closely fought encounter saw Middleton's return to Waterden Road: he scored 10 and the match finished as a 39-39 draw after John Boulger beat Bengt Jansson and Christer Lofqvist in the last heat. England went on to win the competition.

With Hackney's league form as inconsistent as ever, the best hope again seemed the cup and Poole were beaten 45-33 on the 4 August. The next night the Hawks won at Cradley in the league 41-37. The victory was surprising, since Jansson was missing after a workshop accident had left him injured. Home victories followed over Wimbledon

Bengt Jansson in action.

*Hackney, 1972. From left to right: Dave Erskine, Laurie Etheridge, Geoff Maloney,
Barry Thomas, Hugh Saunders, Roger Wright, Dave Kennett, Eddie Reeves, Len Silver.
Bengt Jansson is seated on the bike.*

and Oxford in a double header on 11 August. Oxford were thrashed 60-18. Both
Thomas and Saunders were unbeaten, but for the returning Middleton it was a
nightmare – he scored 1.

Ronnie Moore again won the London Riders Championship on 25 August. His first
victory had been achieved twenty years before in 1952. As the season entered its final
phase, thoughts again turned towards the cup. Reading stood between Hackney and a
place in the final and, as a taster, they rode their British League match at Hackney on 1
September, narrowly losing 41-37. Hackney lost the home league match against Belle
Vue, who were on their way to a third successive league title. Either the Aces or King's
Lynn, who had already won twice at Waterden Road, would face Hackney if they
overcame Reading.

Hackney geared up for the semi-final clash by beating Swedish club Bysarna 52-26,
before taking on Reading in a 22 September double header. Reading were a different
proposition: although Hackney had led by 8 points after heat 8, Reading used tactical
substitutes and went into the last heat 2 points up. Saunders came in to replace
Maloney and he and Thomas rode to a match-winning 5-1, Hackney scraping through
40-38 to face Belle Vue.

The first leg of the final was held at Hackney on 20 October, but the Aces restricted
Hackney to a mere 3-point lead, despite a maximum for Jansson and a solid 9 from

Thomas. Perhaps it was no surprise when Hackney lost the return 33-45 five days later. Jansson scored 12 and Maloney was superb, scoring 10. He recalls:

'At Belle Vue, we used Nitro. I won my first race and next time out I was against Mauger and Alan Wilkisnson. I flew out of the gate – I couldn't believe it and I thought, "Hello, I'm in front of Mauger". For three laps I saw this front wheel coming up the inside of me and I kept chopping it going into the bend. It was only at the end that I realised it was Thommo, and Mauger went round the two of us.'

Finishing as losing cup finalists and eighth in the league was an excellent result for a team that had lost a heat leader and not really replaced him. Jansson scored 4 in the BLRC and, although his scoring was slightly down, he was brilliant again, whilst Thomas continued to improve. Dave Kennett quietly went about his business and finished as third heat leader – his CMA was up two points a match and he had real potential. Despite losing Middleton, there was a combined improvement of the CMAs of Etheridge, Saunders and Reeves, from 15.12 to 18.29. Sometimes a little counts. Much would rest on Thomas and Kennett's ability to improve if honours would be achieved the following year.

During the close season terrible news arrived. On 9 December, former Hawk Jack Biggs was killed in a track crash at Bendigo's Golden City Raceway in Australia. Biggs was riding well but in one race a con-rod broke and blew the engine to pieces. The engine plates were blown out and they dug into the track, stopping the machine and sending Biggs flying into the air. Biggs was fifty years old. His old mate Gooch lamented that 'when he left England he promised me faithfully he wouldn't ride again'.

1972 British League Record (8/18 teams)

Played	Won	Drawn	Lost	For	Against	Pts
34	16	0	18	1,306	1,341	32

1972 Cup Record

Round 1	Bye	
Round 2	Away v. Cradley	Draw 39-39
Round 2	Home v. Cradley	Won 52-26 (replay)
Round 3	Home v. Poole	Won 45-33
Semi-final	Home v. Reading	Won 40-38
Final	H & A v. Belle Vue	Lost 73-82 (aggregate)

1972 British League and Cup Averages (captain in italics)

Rider	Mts	Rds	Pts	BP	Total	CMA	Maxs
Bengt Jansson	*31*	*139*	*316*	*10*	*326*	*9.38*	*7*
Barry Thomas	35	153	278	20	298	7.79	4
Dave Kennett	40	151	195	46	241	6.38	1
Geoff Maloney	34	133	187	23	210	6.32	2
Hugh Saunders	37	139	192	26	218	6.27	2
Laurie Etheridge	40	152	195	42	237	6.24	1
Eddie Reeves	29	101	125	21	146	5.78	
Roger Wright	14	42	36	6	42	4.00	
Allen Emmett	10	25	15	5	20	3.20	

1973 – Another Season, Another Bad Injury

An almost unchanged line-up commenced 1973, with only Eddie Reeves leaving to rejoin Oxford. He was replaced by Allen Emmett. The season opened against King's Lynn in the Spring Gold Cup on 16 March and, as with the previous season, they walked away with a 34-44 victory, Poole managing a draw a week later. This indifferent start to the year was not helped on 30 March when Leicester arrived to open the league campaign. Emmett won his first two rides but what followed was one of the most horrific crashes ever seen at Waterden Road. Emmett sustained a broken thighbone and his career was effectively over; Kennett was badly shaken:

'Alan and I were team riding against Ray Wilson. We were trying to stop him getting past but the handlebars got locked together and we crashed. I ended up on the dog track and he broke his pelvis. It affects your confidence and I was never the same afterwards.'

Hackney managed to win the match 41-37 and signed Dave Kennett's brother, Barney, from Canterbury as a replacement for Emmett.

For the first time the whole cup competition, rather than just the final, was to be run on a home-and-away aggregate basis. Swindon arrived on 27 April, complete with former Hawks Norman Hunter and Brian Leonard, in the first leg of the second round clash and were beaten 43 -35.

A strange incident brought injury to Jansson at Poole on 2 May. The referee had failed to turn up and Hackney and Poole had agreed that the match would proceed with Poole promoter Charles Foot taking charge. Throughout the encounter he did an

Thommo and Banger decide who will challenge for the Golden Helmet.

Barney Kennett.

excellent and fair job, but his inexperience with the controls was to prove costly. Heat 5 saw Hugh Saunders suffer a fall, but Foot placed the red exclusion light on instead of the red stoplights and the riders continued to race and bear down on the prostate Saunders. Jansson, who was leading the race, slowed up but the rider following him, Poole's Odd Fossengen, did not. He ploughed into Banger, knocking him from his bike. It was thought that the only injury was bruised leg muscles and Banger continued in the meeting, which Hackney lost 35-43. However, two nights later at Wolverhampton, Jansson pulled out after only one ride and Hackney were defeated 33-45. The following day, Jansson visited the local hospital and it was discovered that he had broken a bone in his leg. Without Banger, Hackney lost at home to Wimbledon on 11 May, 38-40. But he made an astonishing comeback the next night in the return cup match at Swindon. In a heroic performance, Jansson scored 12 points and, although the Robins won on the night 35-43, it was enough to secure a replay after Hugh Saunders had managed to split the pairing of Edgar Stangeland and Norman Hunter in the final heat.

Newport visited Hackney on 25 May and were soundly beaten 45-33. Barry Thomas and Bengt Jansson were both unbeaten and Thommo won the coin toss for the right to challenge Reidar Eide for the Golden Helmet, which he duly won. Sadly, he was to lose it three nights later to ex-Hawk Roy Trigg in the return match at Newport, which the Hawks also lost 51-27. Hackney beat Swindon in the first leg of the cup replay at Waterden road, the match finishing 43-35 for the third time. Former Hawk Norman Hunter scored 13. Following the meeting, Thomas won the Golden Helmet for the second time after a classic race against Martin Ashby. As before though, he lost it during his first defence – this time against Eric Boocock at Halifax the next night, after Hackney's 49-29 drubbing.

Hackney had a two-week absence from league racing whilst the Daily Mirror International Tournament was held. There had never been such a huge international event, with seven teams taking part in what was essentially a world league. The top four then met in the semi-finals and finals. Hackney hosted two of the qualifying matches. On 29 June, Sweden, skippered by an unbeaten Bengt Jansson, beat the USSR 49-29 and seven days later England took on Poland at Waterden Road. Making his first appearance at Waterden Road was a rider who was destined to play a big part in the future of Hackney – Zenon Plech. The mercurial Pole provided the only real resistance, scoring an impressive 11 points. England won 45-32, helped by Barry Thomas who scored 6. England famously went on to win the final at Wembley after a run-off between Anders Michanek and Peter Collins finished with Michanek excluded after Collins fell.

At the end of July, the Hawks managed to pick up some silverware after beating Wimbledon at home in the second leg of the London Cup and thereby winning on aggregate 82-73. It was soon obvious that that would be all they would win in 1973 as, just twenty-four hours later, the 8-point first-leg lead over Swindon was shown to be totally insufficient and Hackney tumbled out of the Knockout Cup after losing the return by a massive 25-52.

Barney Kennett broke his collarbone in the 28-50 home defeat by Reading on the 3 August and Silver gained permission to sign another foreign rider, eighteen-year-old unknown Swede Tommy Nilsson. Nilsson made his debut against Wolverhampton the following week and scored 4 points and, with Maloney scoring his first British League maximum, the Hawks cruised home 52-26. The injury jinx continued though and Laurie Etheridge was ruled out at King's Lynn on 11 August with a broken leg after a spill at King's Lynn in Hackney's 36-40 defeat. Hackney remain close to the bottom of the table, but Thomas gave the Hawks fans something to cheer when he beat his rival Dave Jessup in a run-off to become London Riders Champion on 21 September. As the season's end approached, Hackney seemed unable to beat anyone, but they didn't lose either. Two draws – at home to bottom club Cradley and also against Sheffield – were split by an away draw at Wimbledon. It was enough to avoid the bottom position and Hackney completed the season in sixteenth place.

Jansson had had a tough season with injury and his average was down on his previous seasons. Perhaps Thomas did not improve as much as could be expected, but he still had the makings of a world-beater and represented Hackney in the BLRC, scoring 5 points. Tommy Nilsson filled the third heat spot and did well, considering his late start to the season. Saunders, Etheridge, Maloney and Dave Kennett saw their averages fall by around a point a match each. In Kennett's case he never really discovered

Tommy Nilsson.

London Riders Champion Barry Thomas, runner-up Dave Jessup and third-placed man Hugh Saunders.

his old form following the crash with Emmett. Although all had their moments, by and large these four did not do as well as the previous year.

Jansson finished in style by winning the very first Champions Chase, but as the close season commenced it was obvious that changes were required. Never in the Hawks fans' wildest dreams would they have guessed what changes would be forced upon them.

1973 British League Record (16/18 teams)

Played	Won	Drawn	Lost	For	Against	Pts
34	11	4	19	1,227	1,421	26

1973 Cup Record

Round 1	Bye	
Round 2	Swindon	Draw 78-78
Round 2	Swindon	Lost 68-87 (replay)

1973 British League and Cup Averages (captain in italics)

Rider	Mts	Rds	Pts	BP	Total	CMA	Maxs
Bengt Jansson	*32*	*121*	*263*	*5*	*268*	*8.86*	*7*
Barry Thomas	38	170	317	16	333	7.84	2
Tommy Nilsson	16	63	87	14	101	6.41	
Dave Kennett	38	142	173	24	197	5.55	
Geoff Maloney	36	144	162	34	196	5.44	1
Hugh Saunders	37	134	154	27	181	5.40	
Laurie Etheridge	30	112	125	23	148	5.29	
Barney Kennett	17	52	48	8	56	4.31	

Champions Chase

Another one of Len Silver's brilliant innovations was the unique 'Champions Chase' meeting. Traditionally, this meeting brought the season to an end and was unique in the fact that thirty-two riders started the event which then proceeded on a knockout basis until the final four raced in the winner-take-all final. The format is not completely dissimilar to the current Grand Prix series, although it has to be acknowledged that this meeting, first run in 1973, was over twenty years ahead of its time. Perhaps the most thrilling element, and one which the Grand Prix organsiers could consider, is the fact that from the very first heat the meeting is sudden death. In every single one of the twenty heats, last place is eliminated. It does not cater for a fall or engine failure – which although harsh, resulted in even more spectacular attempts at avoiding elimination.

The formula is essentially a series of rounds. Round one consists of eight heats, which sees all thirty-two riders compete, with the last placed rider in each heat eliminated. Round two consists of six heats where the surviving twenty-four riders compete, but this time both third and last places are eliminated, leaving just twelve of the original starting line up. Round three, the quarter-finals, are perhaps a little easier, with only four riders eliminated. Three heats take place with first and second places automatically qualifying for the semi-finals, along with the two fastest third places. The first and second riders in the two semi-finals then compete in the winner-take-all final.

Ole Olsen was the undoubted star of Champions Chase, winning three years in a row. The biggest shock came when Hackney reserve Steve Lomas reached the final in 1974, finishing third behind John Louis and second-placed Dave Jessup, but ahead of new World Champion Anders Michanek.

Champions Chase Roll of Honour

1973	Bengt Jansson
1974	John Louis
1975	Ole Olsen
1976	Ole Olsen
1977	Ole Olsen
1978	Dave Jessup
1979	Barry Thomas

The vanquished Anders Michanek and the triumphant Steve Lomas next to television star Jenny Handley, winner John Louis and runner-up Dave Jessup.

HACKNEY HERO

BENGT JANSSON

The Overshadowed Swede

For many Hackney fans, Bengt Jansson is best and most stylish rider ever to have worn the Hackney race-jacket. Every now and then a rider comes along and is simply in the wrong place at the wrong time, and perhaps this is true of Jansson – who in another period may have been World Champion on more than one occasion. But to a certain degree he has been overshadowed by fellow countrymen: Fundin, Knutsson and Michanek, who went just a little further and became World Champion.

Bengt was born on 9 January 1943 in Stockholm (Sweden). He made his British debut for West Ham in 1964 but, despite a solid debut season, did not return to England the following year. 1965 saw Banger's first World Championship performance, scoring a creditable 10 points and finishing in joint fourth place at Wembley. He returned to Britain in 1966 and joined Edinburgh, finishing with a 7.65 CMA. In 1967 he was allocated to Hackney and there began a long and happy association. He was to form a

formidable partnership with Colin Pratt: 'Pratty was a very good rider and Barry Thomas too. I also remember Jackie Biggs, Jimmy Gooch and Malcolm Brown. I could not forget Garry Middleton.'

He scored 11 on his debut against Glasgow, being beaten only by Charlie Monk, and it was only two matches later that he scored his first Hackney maximum in the 48-30 win over West Ham in the Cockney Cup. He finished the season with an impressive 9.87 CMA and scored 12 maximums.

But it was at Wembley in his debut season with the Hawks that he came the closest any Hackney rider would ever come to winning the World Championship title. Bengt's first ride in heat 2 was a tough one against fellow Swedes Fundin and

Michanek and the defending World Champion, Barry Briggs. Four-time winner Fundin had a point to prove, having missed the previous year's final having been suspended during the qualifying rounds and he streaked to victory. But Bengt was tucked into second place, beating the other two major contenders. Two easy wins followed and, after all riders had completed three rides, Bengt had 8 points and was joint third with Russian star Igor Plechanov, trailing the unbeaten Fundin and Ivan Mauger.

Heat 13 saw Plechanov beat Fundin and, with Bengt winning his fourth ride in heat 15 beating Mauger into second place, the scene was set for a thrilling finale with these four riders jointly leading with 11 points. Fundin won his last ride, beating Mauger to guarantee himself at least a run-off and finally killing Mauger's own title aspirations. Bengt needed to win his last ride in the final heat 20 to force a run-off with Fundin, but he was against the other contender Plechanov. Bengt sped from the tapes for a comfortable victory and a place in the run-off for the sport's greatest prize. Englands Eric Boocock relegated Plechanov to third, leaving Mauger automatically with the bronze medal. The run-off was not the thriller that was expected as the fast-starting Fundin easily won, setting a new record of five World Championship victories and leaving Bengt having to be content with second place. Did Banger feel he was robbed of victory?

'Not at all, that's what people say but I wanted to win and Fundin wanted to win too. I only made one gate all night against three Polish boys (heat 5) and all the rest I was last or second from last from the gate. But I passed them – Ivan Mauger, Ray Wilson – I passed them all and I had a really good night.'

The 1968 season saw Banger in the same good form and he won the Silver Sash (precursor of the Golden Helmet) from Barry Briggs, successfully defending it on four occasions against Trevor Hedge, Eddie Reeves Malcolm Simmons, and Anders Michanek, before losing to Neil Street. His partnership with Colin Pratt ensured that Hackney came within a whisker of becoming League Champions, despite his scoring being slightly down on the previous season, finishing with 8.98.

Bengt, like many Swedish riders, did not ride in Britain in 1969 but he returned to the Hawks camp in 1970, scoring 7 maximums on his way to a 9.49 CMA. 1971 was Banger's best year in Hackney colours, helping the Hawks to cup victory. He won the London Riders Championship and again finished on the World Championship rostrum, this time finishing in third place in Gothenburg, behind champion Ole Olsen and Ivan Mauger – who defeated Bengt in a run-off for second place.

In 1972 he became team captain. However, during the season he was to have two lucky escapes. Whilst working in the Hackney workshop there was an explosion that left him with serious burns to his face and hands – 'I was boiling chains at the time and some methanol exploded and I burnt myself'. He was also involved in a mid-air drama on 23 June, while attempting to reach Hackney's away match at Glasgow – 'Somebody went into the toilet and maybe tried to commit suicide there. The plane was diverted to get him out, landing somewhere in Holland'. In the end the match was rained off.

The winter of 1973/74 saw a huge rise in global oil prices and with it came increased air fares. SVEMO, the Swedish controlling body, insisted on their star riders returning home and riding in the Swedish league throughout the year and expected the British League promoters to pay the cost of the fares. The result was that 'commuting foreign' riders were banned from the British League in 1974. Banger still qualified for the World Final, scoring 9 points to finish in joint fourth place with England's Peter Collins and John Louis, but sadly he would never return to ride for Hackney – 'I was disappointed because we wanted to ride in England for our living and also to get into the World Final you had to ride in England in the British League'.

He returned to England in 1975, but lined up at Reading, which was to be Banger's last British team. He rode for the racers for three seasons but his scoring never reached the heights it had done whilst at Waterden Road. He rode in one further World Final, again scoring 9, in the rain-drenched 1977 event in Gothenburg, finishing in sixth place. Banger can explain why he joined up with Reading on his return: 'Len Silver was also at Reading as co-promoter and they wanted me to ride there and I had to go where they wanted me. But I never liked it there, I enjoyed Hackney. Len did everything for the boys and the track was so good. I could ride anywhere. I liked small trick tracks. The last time I went there was the Grand Prix [1995]. Not too good.'

1974 – Banger Banned

The ban on Swedes robbed Hackney of both Jansson and Nilsson. However, the 1973 champions, Reading, were unable to defend their title as their planned move to a new stadium at Smallmead had been delayed and they were forced to sit out the year – leaving their number two Dag Lovaas allocated to Hackney. Lovaas was born in Holmestrand, Norway on 25 February 1951. Both his father, Hilmar, and his brother, Ulf, had won the Norwegian Championship and Dag made it a family trio by winning the title in 1973. His British career started at Newcastle in 1970, where he finished the season with a CMA of 3.91. Following Newcastle's closure at the end of that season, he found himself transferred to Reading, where he made quick progression riding alongside Anders Michanek and finished the 1973 season with a 10.06 CMA.

Hugh Saunders was appointed captain and retained from the previous season were: Laurie Etheridge, Geoff Maloney, Dave Kennett and Barry Thomas. The number seven berth was to be contested between Barney Kennett, Les 'Red' Ott, Allen Emmett and Steve Lomas – who having had second-half rides at Poole signed for Hackney and was loaned out to Weymouth. On the management side, returning to Hackney in the role of team coach was former Hackney star Colin Pratt.

The traditional opening night team was King's Lynn who, for the third year running, emerged with the Spring Gold Cup, winning 36-42 on 15 March. Cradley and Coventry were both dispatched in the British League and a draw was gained at Wolverhampton. However, Poole dumped the Hawks out of the cup and Silver strengthened the team

Dave Morton.   *A young Zenon Plech.*

by signing Dave Morton. Born on 24 September 1953, Morton had had second-half rides at Belle Vue before joining Crewe in 1971 and had made good progress in the Second Division, finishing the 1973 season with a 8.44 CMA. Silver was part of a consortium promoting at Crewe and therefore had ample opportunity to weigh up Morton's ability. He had ridden in four matches for Hackney the previous season but had been reluctant to sign permanently for the team, due to the 400-mile round trip for each home match. Morton started scoring well from the start and his arrival signalled a purple patch for the Hawks. His home debut was against Hull on 24 May, scoring 6 points, and he raced to a maximum against Wimbledon the following week.

Hackney scored their first-ever away win at Oxford, winning 44-34 on 6 June. This left them sitting on the top of the table, but it was to be short-lived. Title favourites Exeter arrived on 14 June and, despite missing Ivan Mauger on long-track duty, emerged victorious 38-40 after Falcons' guest Terry Betts completed his maximum and beat Lovaas in the last heat. The Hawks were 10 points up after eight heats and let the match slip from their grasp disappointingly, since twenty-four hours later the Hawks went to Cradley and thrashed the home team 49-29.

Despite the disagreements between England and Sweden, a test series took place and Hackney hosted the fourth test on 21 June. By then England had already sewn up victory, having won the first three tests with only Soren Sjosten providing any resistance. Perhaps something can be read into the fact that the Swedes failed to track some of their best riders – including Michanek, Bernie Persson and Christer Lofqvist.

Barry Thomas was called up to ride for England and scored 9 points in England's 73-35 victory and the meeting also gave Hackney fans a chance to welcome back Bengt Jansson, although he only scored 5.

The Hawks continued to perform well and beat Wolverhampton at Waterden Road by 49-29 on 5 July. Morton's form was nothing short of sensational and he beat Ole Olsen twice that night on his way to a 12-point maximum.

It was back to test match action the following week as Hackney staged the first test against Poland, including the return of Zenon Plech – who had impressed so much during the previous season's test. However he could only manage 3 points and the Poles were thrashed 88-19, losing the first sixteen heats 5-1. In fact the only thing that saved Poland from a whitewash was a fall in heat 17 for the England skipper Ray Wilson. Thomas again rode for England and, like most of his team-mates, was unbeaten.

Apart from Morton's good form, Lovaas was also proving a revelation and was scoring above 10 points per match. He was rewarded by being nominated to challenge John Louis in the Golden Helmet Match Race Championship. Ipswich visited on 19 July and Lovaas won his only meeting with Louis. The Hawks' title hopes suffered another dent though, as the Witches won 30-47. It was the beginning of the end of Hackney's championship challenge.

During the next week, away losses were suffered at Poole and Wimbledon and, to complete a miserable eight days, King's Lynn narrowly won at the Wick on 26 July, 38-40. The Stars' Terry Betts, in a repeat of his guest performance for Exeter, beat Lovaas in the last heat. To add insult to injury, Louis beat Lovaas 2-0 in the Golden Helmet at the start of the meeting. Despite heat leaders Lovaas, Thomas and Morton scoring well, the remainder of the team were very up and down and Hackney lost their way.

Belle Vue won 37-41 on 30 August, despite a Lovaas 12-point maximum. That night another new signing was announced, 'Hurricane' Ted Hubbard. Born on 20 June 1949, Hubbard had made his debut for Canterbury in 1970 and had progressed to be an accomplished Second Division performer. He would go on to be closely associated with the Hawks. Like Morton at Crewe and Lomas at Weymouth, he would complete the season at the Kent track and a few weeks after his signature finished second in the Second Division Rider's Championship.

The following week, as Hackney relinquished the London Cup to Wimbledon, Lovaas was making his one and only appearance in the World Final in Gothenberg. He scored 6 points to finish in joint tenth place. Lovaas' experience of speedway's big night may have made him favourite for the following week's London Riders Championship, but it was team-mate Thomas that retained his title with a 15-point maximum.

The Hawks finally finished in ninth place in the league table. Lovaas had been the year's star rider, scoring 3 in the BLRC. Morton had been a revelation with an impressive average of 6.34 and splitting them was Thomas, who still had not realised his full potential. There was little to choose between Skipper Saunders, Etheridge, Maloney or Kennett – all had averages around the 5-point mark. Lomas looked like he could be a good prospect and finished the season third in the Champions Chase.

It was unclear what the following season was going to bring. Would the Swedes return and, if so, would it be Lovaas or Janssen that led Hackney?

1974 British League Record (9/17 teams)

Played	Won	Drawn	Lost	For	Against	Pts
32	13	2	17	1,218	1,273	28

1974 Cup Record

Round 1	Poole	Lost 76-80

1974 British League and Cup Averages (captain in italics)

Rider	Mts	Rds	Pts	BP	Total	CMA	Maxs
Dag Lovaas	29	127	321	2	323	10.17	6
Barry Thomas	33	145	265	17	282	7.78	2
Dave Morton	26	99	147	10	157	6.34	2
Steve Lomas	9	34	40	9	49	5.77	
Hugh Saunders	*34*	*131*	*144*	*32*	*176*	*5.37*	
Laurie Etheridge	34	131	144	32	176	5.37	
David Kennett	25	84	93	19	112	5.33	
Geoff Maloney	32	99	82	29	111	4.49	

1975 – The Lofqvist Twist

1975 was to be remembered as the season of Christer Lofqvist. He had been a firm favourite in London's East End when riding for West Ham in 1970 and 1971. After the Hammers' closure he moved to Poole, where he reached his first World Final in 1972, finishing a creditable fourth place with 11 points. Dag Lovaas had moved to Oxford and, with Bengt Janssen returning to England but with Reading rather than Hackney, Lofqvist was signed as his replacement. He had reached his second World Final in 1974, this time finishing in joint seventh place with 8 points. From the start his relationship with Silver was stormy and it would get worse.

Skipper Hugh Saunders had retired after a poor season and was replaced by Mike Broadbank, signed from Stoke. Broadbank was forty years old, having started his career at Rye House in 1955 in the Southern League before moving on to Wembley. But it was at Swindon where he spent the best years of his career, riding alongside Barry Briggs. He had reached seven World Finals (two as reserve), but had always finished at the lower end of the score chart. His best result was achieved in 1964, when he finished in joint ninth with 6 points. Broadbank was also London Riders Champion in 1964. Another long-serving Hawk, Laurie Etheridge, was loaned to Crayford – having also struggled in 1974 – and was replaced by Ted Hubbard. Completing the line-up was Dave Morton (stepping up full-time into the British League from Crewe), Steve Lomas (recalled from Weymouth) and the sole survivors from the previous season – Dave Kennett and Barry Thomas (who was appointed as the new captain).

Christer Lofqvist.

Veteran Mike Broadbank.

The home season started with a British League encounter against Newport on 14 March. Missing star man Phil Crump, the Welsh side succumbed easily 45-33. The Spring Gold Cup commenced and the Hawks managed to beat King's Lynn home and away, but this good work was undone a week later when Ipswich won at Hackney 38-40. Worse was to follow on Sunday 13 April. Hackney travelled to Second Division Boston in the first round of the all-new inter-league Knockout Cup. This competition saw British League clubs visiting Second Division teams in the first round, continuing with single-leg matches to the two-legged final – similar to the old-style competition. Against all the odds, the Baracudas pulled off a shock giant-killing performance, winning 38-40. Whilst there may have been some mitigating circumstances behind the defeat – such as Lofqvist being absent and Barry Thomas grinding to a halt in the last race – it was still a shock defeat.

A win at Wolverhampton atoned in part for the cup upset and was followed by a narrow victory over Exeter, despite Lofqvist being an unexplained absentee. However, all was not well in the Hawks camp. Seven away defeats followed, as well as a home defeat against Oxford. Cradley provided the opposition at Waterden Road on 13 June and were soundly beaten 58-20 to bring the lean spell to a temporary end. Thomas and Morton were both immaculate with 12-point maximums and Lofqvist was also unbeaten, scoring 8 paid 12.

A week later and the Hawks were narrowly defeated at Wimbledon 40-38, despite the fact that Lofqvist was again mysteriously absent. A consolation for Hackney was that Barry Thomas became the new Plough Lane track record holder. The first sign of the coming storm came on 27 June when Leicester visited in the cup. Silver commented: 'The question on everyone's lips in the East End of London at the moment is, where is Christer? Of course it may well be that there is a perfectly reasonable explanation for his "disappearance" and that he may turn up this evening ready and raring.' He didn't, and the Hawks were restricted to a 2-point lead in the first leg and, not surprisingly, four days later Hackney's cup hopes were over when they lost the return match 31-47.

Lofqvist returned to ride in the London Riders Championship on 4 July, which was won by Dave Jessup, and a week later Hackney staged the third England versus Sweden test match. Both Thomas and Morton were selected for the England team and Lofqvist was called up for Sweden. England emerged as victors 62-46 on their way to a 5-0 series

'Hurricane' Ted Hubbard.

win and Lofqvist top scored for Sweden with 11 points. By the time of the fifth test at Belle Vue just five days later, Lofqvist had quit and never rode for Hackney again. Without the Swede, Hackney lost at home on 18 July – ironically to Lofqvist's former club, Poole – 36-42.

Wimbledon were the following week's visitors and Silver wrote in his programme notes: 'The weary episode of Lofqvist has caused me more pain than any previous experience of promoting I can remember. For what seemed no apparent reason he took a personal dislike to me, and frankly I was pleased when he finally told me, at Belle Vue, that not only did he not wish to ride for Hackney, he no longer wished to ride in the British League. He let us down very badly, refusing offers of mechanical assistance and continually using and testing untried equipment during our important league and cup events.' Less than three years later Lofqvist was dead, the result of a brain tumour. Ted Hubbard recalls his team-mate:

'Christer Lofqvist was my partner for a while. He was funny bloke sometimes, he had a brain tumour and he may have been suffering already. Once we were at Belle Vue and we had a drink afterwards and Christer was there. There were some Belle Vue supporters who cut up a bit funny and Christer turn round and said "Don't worry, I will kill him with one hand", I said to Thommo "I hope he knows what he's doing or I'm off!"'

But there was a ray of hope on the horizon to finish the season. By mid-September, Hackney had signed the so-called 'Golden Boy of Polish Speedway' Zenon Plech. It was to be one of Hackney's best signings. Plech made his debut at home to Wolverhampton in a match, which featured Wolverhampton's Danish star Finn Thomsen – later to be a team-mate of Plech's. Hackney were winning again, helped by Dave Kennett – who beat Ole Olsen from the back in heat 10, inflicting the new World Champion's only defeat. Plech scored a solid 8 points. Wimbledon won the first leg of the London Cup at Plough Lane on 16 October, 30-48, and Hackney just failed to pull back the deficit on 24 October, winning on the night 46-32.

Plech arrived too late to make much difference to Hackney's league position, but provided a much-needed boost to the team morale as the season came to an end. Hackney finished in seventeenth place with just Swindon below them, having lost all their away matches following the early season win at Wolves and losing half of their home matches too.

Morton continued his excellent progress and topped the averages over 2 points up on the previous season. Thomas finished second and had proved an excellent new captain, although now in his sixth season at Hackney still had not reached the dizzy heights predicted for him. Lofqvist only rode in 12 matches and his scoring in those was disappointing. Apart from the lack of a third heat leader, the Hackney tail-end had proved disappointing too. Kennett, Lomas and Broadbank all finished with averages around the 4-point mark. Hubbard, who had been plagued with bumps and knocks, had shown flashes of form that hinted that he could make it in the senior league. The key to a better 1976 would undoubtedly rest on Plech's availability.

1975 British League Record (17/18 teams)

Played	Won	Drawn	Lost	For	Against	Pts
34	9	1	24	1,221½	1,429½	19

1975 Cup Record

Round 1	Leicester	Lost 71-84

1975 British League and Cup Averages (captain in italics)

Rider	Mts	Rds	Pts	BP	Total	CMA	Maxs
Dave Morton	32	141	297	4	301	8.54	4
Barry Thomas	*36*	*169*	*317*	*13*	*330*	*7.81*	*2*
Christer Lofqvist	12	51	84	13	97	7.61	1
Laurie Etheridge	14	50	60	13	73	5.84	1
David Kennett	36	130	128	24	152	4.68	
Steve Lomas	34	120	113	25	138	4.60	
Mike Broadbank	36	114	106	21	127	4.46	
Ted Hubbard	28	85	72	10	82	3.86	

[Zenon Plech 7.11 (4 matches only)]

1976 – Silver Banned

Quiet optimism signalled the commencement of the 1976 season – and not without good reason. With last season's stars Dave Morton and Zenon Plech back and Barry Thomas completing the heat leaders, Hackney looked at least as though their top end would be the match of most others. Also retained were Dave Kennett and Steve Lomas. Mike Broadbanks joined Crayford and Ted Hubbard was loaned to Rye House (who had moved en bloc from Rayleigh in 1974). Replacing these two were riders at either end of their career. Ex-Hawk Trevor Hedge returned for the first time since 1963.

Born on 3 August 1943, Hedge had established himself as a star at Wimbledon, where he rode for nine seasons, forming a formidable partnership with double World Champion Ronnie Moore. He had himself qualified for the World Final in 1970 as England's sole representative, but failed to score on a night when every conceivable piece of bad luck beset him. When still only thirty-two, he completed the 1975 season at King's Lynn with a 6.20 CMA.

Born in Hackney on 27 August 1956, the son of former rider Vic, Keith White had started his career at Peterborough in 1972 before signing for Leicester and joining Crewe on loan. 'I'd ridden for Len at Crewe for a couple of years and then I went to Birmingham and my dad was at Leicester and it didn't seem right to be in the same team so I went back to Len at Hackney. I was born about two miles from the stadium.' He had doubled up with Leicester in the 1975 season, scoring an impressive 4.92 CMA in his British League debut season. His potential was huge and Hackney had great expectations for him.

The season commenced at Reading on 15 March in atrocious conditions, where only Barry Thomas got the grips with the track conditions, scoring 13 points and beating both Bengt Jansson and John Davies from the back. London speedway had been boosted by the addition of a third track, through the return of White City, and that gave added spice to the Spring Gold Cup competition. Hackney beat the West London team 41-37 the following week, but disaster struck in the return at White City just five days later when Trevor Hedge was ruled out with a seriously gashed knee after a clash with ex-Hawk Dag Lovaas; it would be months before he returned. To add insult to injury, Hawks succumbed 42-36. 'I got out the start and into the first corner and Dag's bike hit me, apparently he had reared coming out of the start and jumped off the back of the bike that just careered into me. I had to have fifty-three stitches in my leg. He retired as a result of that, it upset him so much.'

Having won at Wolverhampton, Hackney also stole a win at Leicester, 42-36, on 11 May. Morton was again the architect of the victory with a 12-point maximum and guest Tony Featherstone scored a vital 9 points. Just four days later, Hackney lost at Swindon and Silver was in hot water. He visited the referees' box during the 35-42 defeat and at the subsequent tribunal he was banned from promoting for a month. He spent the whole of July unable to legally participate in the match or write programme notes.

Zenon Plech scored his first paid maximum in the home 43-35 win over Wolverhampton on 25 June, but his second was even better. Belle Vue visited on 23 July and became the first team to take points away from the Wick, winning 40-38. Plech was unbeaten, but in doing so beat Peter Collins twice in two epic encounters with repeated passing throughout. The match was essentially lost in heat 12 when Thomas fell whilst battling with Collins and trying to join Plech up front for a match winning 5-1.

With Silver returning to the management fray, more drama was around the corner. With the country sizzling under a major heat wave, tempers were about to boil over. Reading arrived on 6 August and an exciting match ensued. Heat 11 saw Dave Morton and Steve Lomas line up against Dave Jessup and Boleslaw Proch with the match finely balanced at 30-30. Jessup was excluded for unfair riding and Reading walked out of the meeting. The re-run and the following two heats were all completed with the two Hackney riders only and the resulting 5-0s saw the Hawks win 45-30.

As the season entered its final stage, the Hawks secured their third away win of the season by winning at Wimbledon 39-38, but the following night failed to establish a large lead in the first leg of the cup clash with Halifax, winning by just 4 points – this was mainly due to Plech's absence riding the World Final. There was high hopes that,

Keith White.

14th Season

MEETING No.	FRIDAY, AUGUST 6th, 1976 at 8.00 p.m.	
	Gulf Oil British League	Magazine
21	*v.* **READING**	Programme
		Value 20p

Plus STANDARD MOTORISTS' CENTRES GOLDEN HELMET MATCH RACE

1976 programme.

Hackney, 1976. From left to right, back row: Zenon Plech, Barry Thomas, Dave Morton. Front row: Trevor Hedge, Keith White, Steve Lomas, Dave Kennett.

in his home country, Plech may bring back the crown, having finished in third place the last time the final was held at Katowice. However, a poor first race saw him pegged back to joint fourth place with 11 points as England's Peter Collins stormed to victory.

The Hawks tumbled out of the cup when the return was staged at Halifax on 18 September, losing 31-47, but a last-gasp away win again at Reading on 18 October, 43-35, saw the Hawks finish in a respectable seventh position in the final British League table, with only Champions Ipswich and second place Belle Vue winning at Waterden Road.

As neither Wimbledon nor White City had spare dates available, the London Cup was decided at Hackney on 22 October. Hackney would race firstly Wimbledon and then White City, with Hackney's accumulative score divided by two to find the champions. Wimbledon won the first match 29-49 and secured the title after Hackney beat the Rebels in the second match 42-36.

Dave Morton had hit the big time, finishing with a final CMA in excess of 10 points and scoring 4 points in the BLRC. Plech had shown he too was a rider of world-class ability, but his equipment was undoubtedly losing him many points both in lack of horsepower and breakdowns. Thomas was the reliable third heat leader and White had a satisfactory first season. Perhaps the reason for Hackney's failure to finish a bit higher was the team's lack of strength in depth. Hedge had a nightmare year, and his CMA suffered accordingly, while Dave Kennett could not recover past glories and Steve Lomas simply failed to impress. With a top four that could – and almost certainly would – do better, the progress made in 1976 could be built upon.

1976 British League Record (7/18 teams)

Played	Won	Drawn	Lost	For	Against	Pts
36	20	0	16	1,392	1,404	40

1976 Cup Record

Round 1	Reading	Won 81-75
Round 2	Halifax	Lost 74-82

1976 British League and Cup Averages (captain in italics)

Rider	Mts	Rds	Pts	BP	Total	CMA	Maxs
Dave Morton	36	154	386	6	392	10.18	7
Zenon Plech	36	147	268	23	291	7.92	2
Barry Thomas	*39*	*165*	*239*	*36*	*275*	*6.67*	
Keith White	40	165	231	30	261	6.33	1
Laurie Etheridge	14	53	58	15	73	5.51	
Trevor Hedge	24	82	83	27	110	5.37	
Steve Lomas	34	97	99	21	120	4.95	
Ted Hubbard	7	25	25	5	30	4.80	
Dave Kennett	40	130	114	22	136	4.19	

1977 – Pole-Axed

18 March was the opening night of the 1977 season. As the fans filed into the stadium and read their programmes, it was apparent that things had already started to go wrong. Not at Waterden Road though, but in Stal Gorzow, Poland, the home club of Zenon Plech. The sporting politics in the country at this time are likely to remain a mystery but someone, somewhere in Poland – be it a club official or someone in the government – was about to ruin Hackney's season before it even started. Len Silver commented in the opening night's programme notes: 'The big question everyone is asking is will Zenon Plech be back? And I scratch my head and say I hope so.' Having not being able to secure agreement from his Polish club to return to England for the new season, Plech had requested a transfer, which so incensed the authorities that they slapped a two-year international ban on him. Silver still retained hopes that Plech would return – particularly as Stal Gorzow were on tour in England and due at Hackney just one week later.

So the opening night battle against King's Lynn in the Spring Gold Cup was fought without one of the heat leaders, using rider replacement in Plech's place. Making up the rest of the team retained from the previous season were: Thomas, Morton, White, Lomas, and Hedge and, based on a good guest performance from the previous season, Tony Featherstone was signed from Peterborough, replacing Dave Kennett. At the end of the rain soaked night there was every reason to believe that the season would indeed be rosy after a narrow 41-37 victory. Morton had scored an impressive 16, Thomas and White had provided strong backing and, despite no Plech, rider replacement had brought in 9 points.

The following week Stal Gorzow arrived, minus Plech. A poor display saw them thrashed 56-22 with only a solid 9 from Jerzy Rembas preventing an even worse massacre. It was not until the Superama programme notes on 22 April that the matter was addressed again, with Silver admitting that he was now pursuing a replacement in parallel with continuing to locate and get Plech released. That rider was eventually revealed as Jerzy Rembas. A week later and the Polish Motor Federation was reported as

Tony Featherstone.

meeting to decide Plech's fate, with the outcome being that Plech signed for Gorzow and that he would now be available to return to the Hackney side.

Hackney's league campaign commenced with two away defeats, 38-40 at Wolverhampton and the following night 24-54 at Halifax, where, after a distinguished career, Hedge had finally had enough: 'I remember packing up. We were at Halifax that night and they kept cheating out of the start, it was pouring down with rain, the track was black granite and if you missed the start that was it. I was a bit cheesed off and that was it, I never rode again.'

On 4 May Hackney were thrashed at White City 17-61. The match was controversial as Morton, who had arrived early, had been told that the match was rained off and so he returned home, leaving Hackney to their fate. Two nights later Poole were the visitors. Silver had given up all hope of securing Plech for the season. In the latest twist he had been drafted into the Polish Army and although he was free to continue riding it would have to be for a club near his army base and that club was Gdansk. Silver was

Bent Rasmussen.

Thommo, cigarette in hand.

under no illusion that there was a sinister plot behind the wheeling and dealings and so, as the Hawks prepared to face Poole, Plech was at last abandoned. Poole had recently lost Kevin Holden, who had been tragically killed in a track crash at the Wimborne Road circuit, but they still tracked a competitive side, led by the current world number two, Malcolm Simmons. All began well with the in-form Morton beating Simmons in the first race, but heat 6 was to prove disastrous. Morton comfortably led his third ride when he appeared to pick up grip coming out of turn two. His bike took off into the air before crashing again onto the track, bouncing along the back straight and into the safety fence. It was a horrific accident and for Morton the season was over, his right leg having been badly broken.

By the end of May absolutely nothing had gone right for Hackney and the road ahead looked very hard indeed with rider replacement for Plech and guests for Morton. The unknown Dane Bent Rasmussen had been signed as replacement for Hedge and was notching up some impressive scores and Ted Hubbard returned to the Hackney side with some impressive home performances, after patience with the struggling Lomas had finally run out and he was transferred to Wovlerhampton.

Even more significant was Hackney's signing of Vic Harding from Weymouth. Vic made his home debut on 22 July against Coventry – a match which was to prove one of the most controversial of the season.

Coventry had led for most of the encounter and, with the last heat to go, were 4 points in front. Hackney's chances of a draw rested on guest Doug Wyer and skipper Barry Thomas. Standing in there way though was the unbeaten former World Champion Ole Olsen and the equally impressive ex-Hawk Tommy Nilsson. The green light came on and, strangely, Olsen moved away from the tapes and returned to the pits. After much debate and flaring tempers, the race was started without either Coventry rider, who declined to start, leaving Thomas and Wyer to ride around unopposed for a match, thereby winning 5-0. Olsen stormed out of the meeting. The fact that the green light was already on should in itself have earned Olsen exclusion once he pulled back, but even more strangely was the fact that the likelihood of Hackney getting the required 5-1 for a draw was quite remote. Later in the season, the result was amended to 35-39 after Coventry appealed over the use of Wyer in heats 11 and 13.

A disappointing season finally came to an end with Hackney incredibly avoiding the wooden spoon. The main source of good news was the scoring of Keith White, who had risen to the occasion and moved into the vacant number one slot with a string of impressive performances – scoring 10 points in the British Final, he reaching the penultimate round of the World Championship, the Intercontinental Final. Before the season's end Dave Morton had requested a transfer, but there was still reason for quiet optimism for the future. Bent Rasmussen, Vic Harding and a young Danish youngster called Bo Petersen were signed for the following season and everything looked set for a bright future. Thomas too, although typically not scoring as well as he should have, was at his entertaining best and, as the season progressed, was adding to his tally of big-name scalps: Michael Lee, John Louis and Terry Betts all saw Thommo's back wheel during the season, but the biggest scalp of all came on Friday 30 September when the Exeter Falcons hit town.

The race that made the newspapers.

Ivan Mauger, the newly crowned World Champion, had just equalled Ove Fundin's record of five World Championship victories and Exeter was slugging it out with White City for the League Championship. Hackney had shrewdly booked the Rebels' Gordon Kennett as a guest for Morton, but it was Thomas and White that led the charge and Hackney had developed a 10-point lead by the halfway stage. The Falcons hit back and lined up for the all-important heat 13 needing a 1-5 to draw the match and keep the championship alive.

White and Thomas lined up for Hackney, Mauger and the American Scott Autrey for Exeter. The tapes rose and the Exeter pair raced to the front with wheel-perfect team riding. Autrey hugged the white line and Mauger was out wide, thwarting both Thomas' and White's efforts as the Hackney pair tried everything to get past over three-and-half fantastic laps. On the last corner, Thommo swept round the kickboards, squeezing through the smallest of gaps between a shocked

NO CATCHING SUPER BARRY

HACKNEY speedway skipper Barry Thomas virtually ended Exeter's chances of snatching the British League title last night.

Thomas flew past the Exeter pairing of world champion Ivan Mauger and Scott Autrey to win the last heat and seal a 41-37 victory at Hackney Stadium.

Maximum points in that race would have given Exeter a draw, but now they have little hope of catching leaders White City.

Thomas and team-mate Keith White both finished with 13 points.

Mauger and the safety fence to win the race, the meeting 41-37 for Hackney and effectively the League Championship for White City. For all Hawks fans this race and the pass that made it so memorable were to become Hackney folklore and be regarded by many as the greatest race of all time at the famous East London circuit.

1977 British League Record (16/19 teams)

Played	Won	Drawn	Lost	For	Against	Pts
36	13	1	22	1,256½	1,537½	27

1977 Cup Record

Round 1	Sheffield	Won 81-75
Round 2	King's Lynn	Lost 70-86

1977 British League and Cup Averages (captain in italics)

Rider	Mts	Rds	Pts	BP	Total	CMA	Maxs
Keith White	40	211	379	14	393	7.45	4
Barry Thomas	*39*	*209*	*295*	*45*	*340*	*6.51*	
Ted Hubbard	8	29	37	9	46	6.35	
Bent Rasmussen	29	117	123	14	137	4.68	
Vic Harding	19	63	55	11	66	4.19	
Tony Featherstone	38	114	95	21	116	4.07	
Laurie Etheridge	11	33	27	5	32	3.88	
Steve Lomas	14	44	25	6	31	2.82	

[Also Dave Morton 8.67 (5 matches only)]

Fifty Glorious Years
The Golden Jubilee Meeting
19 February 1978

Speedway's first ever meeting in this country was held at High Beech in Epping Forest on 19 February 1928, with a reported 30,000 people in attendance. The exploits of Galloway, MacKay, Creek and Barnett on that day have been fully documented, but little has been recorded about the meeting, exactly fifty years later, which celebrated speedway's birth in England. Hackney had the honour of staging this event, which was to be staged outside the normal season, exactly fifty years to the day on 19 February 1978. Before describing the action, it is necessary to mention what is probably most people's recollection of that day – the weather. Although dry, it was perhaps the coldest that people could remember. Certainly the coldest day on which they had ever watched speedway – and the event was not short.

It started with a grand parade featuring pioneer members of the Veteran Dirt-track Riders Association, current stars who were participating in the meeting and, of course, the man credited with starting it all – Johnnie Hoskins. Throughout the day interviews and attractions tried to keep the cold fans' spirits high and it was not long before they were enjoying the first action: a match race between the legendary Jack Parker, by now well into his seventies, and current star Malcolm Simmons. Parker had been renowned as a match-race specialist in his day – so much so that the Golden Helmet Match Race

If you ignore the modern-day Kelvin Mullarkey, you would be forgiven for thinking that leg-trailing Barry Thomas is in the wrong era! Note the crowd size too.

Championship was nicknamed 'Parker's Pension'. Parker rode a modern-day machine whilst Simmons was riding an old Douglas. Parker certainly remembered how to make a lightning start and, still looking surprisingly sprightly, led Simmons for four laps to a popular victory.

The main event was a traditional 20-heat individual meeting, but with each set of four heats the riders were to ride period machines in the style of the era and the races were to start in the tradition of the time.

Heats 1 to 4 were to feature machines from 1928 until 1930, leg trailing and the starts were to be rolling – each rider keeping in line until they went over the start/finish line when the race would automatically begin. Heats 5 to 8 were to feature machines from the mid-1930s, leg-trailing and the races were to start using the standing flag start technique. Heats 9 to 12 were to feature machines from the late 1940s to mid-1960s, leg-trailing or foot forward, and a starting gate clutch start. Heats 13 to 16 were to feature machines from the late 1960s, foot forward, again with a clutch start. Heats 17 to 20 brought things right up to date with contemporary machines.

Sadly, the weather was to play an important role. Such was the bitterness of the cold that many of the old machines simply refused to start and such was the delay and uncertainty of their ongoing performance, it was reluctantly decided that all the heats would have to use modern bikes. This was a terrible shame, but all was not lost. The starting techniques were still followed and several riders, dressed in old black leathers and period goggles, tried very hard to put on a vintage performance. None more so than Hackney skipper Barry Thomas, who even dropped his handlebars to aid his leg-trailing demonstration. Thommo looked every part the hero of bygone days and won the Most Authentic Rider award – treating the crowd to an exhibition of leg trailing not seen for many a year. He remembers: 'I really enjoyed that. I never had any practice doing it and I thought I'm going to do it and if the others are going cheat, well so be it. I was amazed how many I got and that I beat some of them blokes riding that way, I should have been born earlier!'

Once the decision was taken to use modern bikes, there was only going to be one winner. King's Lynn's up-and-coming Michael Lee rode to victory, scoring 14 points. Despite the stubbornness of the old machines and the cold weather, speedway celebrated its first fifty years in style.

Golden Jubilee of British Speedway Results:

Michale Lee 14, Kelvin Mullarkey 12, Eric Broadbelt 12, Vic Harding 12, Mick Hines 11, Trevor Geer 8, Barry Thomas 7, Bobby McNeil 7, Malcolm Simmons 5, Ted Hubbard 5, Terry Betts 5, Paul Gachet 5, Laurie Etheridge 3, Ray Wilson 1, Tony Featherstone 0, Karl Fiala (reserve) 7, Bob Garrad (reserve) 6.

1978 – Unhappiness is 38-40

High hopes existed for the 1978 season and, significantly for Hackney, they made a signing that was to transpire as one of their best ever. Morton was released in a swap deal with Wolverhampton, which brought to Hackney a rider that was to prove one of the most popular that had donned their race-jacket. Finn Thomsen was born on 16 February 1955 in Ulkaer, Denmark. He was Danish Junior Champion in 1973 and, having attended an Ole Olsen training school in England, decided to further his career in the British League, signing for Wolverhampton in 1974 where he finished with a 4.28 CMA. He rode for the Wolves for a further three seasons, overcoming a serious broken leg in 1976 to finish as world number five just twelve months later in 1977. He came to Hackney with an 8.17 CMA.

Joining him was Bobby McNeil from Swindon. McNeil was born on 27 February 1955 in Canterbury, Kent. He made his debut for Eastbourne in 1971 and scored a creditable 6.82. He went on to ride for the Eagles for another three seasons, finishing top of the averages in both 1973 and 1974. Having had some British League experience with Reading and Oxford, he made the switch to the top flight with Swindon in 1975, where he stayed until joining Hackney with a 6.67 CMA. Thomas, White, Harding, Rasmussen and Petersen completed the line-up, with Tony Featherstone transferred to Kent neighbours Crayford.

The opening results were steady rather than spectacular: an opening night draw with Ipswich and narrow home victories for both sides on the Good Friday home and away clashes with champions White City. For many fans the visit of Hull on 14 April was eagerly anticipated. Ivan Mauger had transferred to Hull during the winter and many fans were still enjoying Thomas' heat 13 victory over Mauger the previous season. They were not disappointed as Thomas did it again, once more beating Mauger in heat 13, to deliver the World Champion's only defeat of the night. Unfortunately, Thomsen came last and Hull won 38-40.

The problem seemed to be that Thomsen was struggling to adapt to the Waterden Road circuit, although away from home he was scoring well – including a 12-point maximum at his former track, Wolverhampton. It was Bobby McNeil and Vic Harding who were giving the fans the most cause to cheer with consistently good scores, but on 1 June McNeil broke his collarbone in the away thrashing at Wimbledon. Fortunately, McNeil's average meant that Hackney could use rider replacement and, with White relegated to the reserve berth, there was still hope that Hackney would begin to climb the table. After an encouraging first year, Bent Rasmussen more often than not failed to live up to expectations and he moved to King's Lynn in a swap with fellow struggler Billy Spiers – a move that was unpopular with the fans.

Hackney's second away victory came on 16 July at sister track Rye House in the inter-league Knockout Cup – a match notable for two reasons. One of them was that Bo Petersen scored the first of what would become many full maximums for the Hawks, the other was a rare run-in with a referee for Barry Thomas.

Unbeaten, he lined up for his last race in heat 12. The tapes rose and Thomas hit the front, but was run into by Rye number one Ted Hubbard, causing Thomas to fall. To everyone's astonishment, referee and former rider Reg Trott excluded Thomas. Hubbard immediately admitted that it was his fault, but Thomas' white exclusion light stayed on. Thommo recalls: 'I punched the light out. I said to Chalkey White "Come over to the light and I'll get onto your shoulders and I'll put it out". I hit it once and it didn't go out but the second time I hit it, it did! Colin Pratt was not very impressed.' Thomas was still excluded and earned a fine for his trouble, which was easily paid off by an impromptu collection by the fans.

Bobby McNeil returned from injury, but his scores showed that he was clearly far from fit and he was forced to sit on the sidelines again whilst his shoulder fully recovered. Indifferent results continued and Thomsen organised a secret practice session for the whole team to experiment with machinery and racing lines. In a further attempt to secure higher scores, Silver arranged for the former Stamford Bridge star and designer of the first Jap engine, Wal Phillips, to join the team as technical advisor.

Hackney staged the fifth and final test match against Australasia on 18 August. Barry Thomas was selected to ride as first reserve. In heat 6 Malcolm Simmons was excluded but England manager John Berry used the second reserve, Tony Davey, who rode for Berry at Ipswich, to replace him. Davey trailed home last. The match was closely fought and, with one heat to go, England were ahead 53-49. Gordon Kennett had struggled

Hackney, 1978. From left to right: Vic Harding, Finn Thomsen, Bent Rasmussen, Bo Petersen, Bobby McNeil, Keith White. Barry Thomas is seated on the bike.

The late Vic Harding.

and Berry earned the jeers of the Hackney crowd by again using Davey as a replacement, leaving home hero Thomas without a ride. Berry's decision was somewhat vindicated, however, as Davey won the race and secured England's 56-52 victory.

25 August brought both Wolverhampton and Hull to town in a double header. It was the first time Dave Morton had returned to the Wick since his crash the previous season. He was a shadow of the rider he was before that incident and Wolves were easily beaten. In the second match, Hackney's run in the inter-league cup continued with victory against Hull in the quarter-final. Hull were without Mauger and, by the end of the night, they had lost American star Kelly Moran after a horrific crash in heat 8 with Bobby McNeil. The two riders tangled approaching the starting gate and were hit by Moran's team-mate Robbie Gardner – all three riders crashed across the line. McNeil walked away, while Moran sustained a fractured pelvis and shoulder. Replacing Spiers, Malcolm Shakespeare, a new signing from Weymouth, endeared himself to the crowd by the way he rode in the re-run, clearly helping a badly shaken McNeil in an attempt to give him a confidence-boosting win.

Wal Phillips was taking a particular interest in Vic Harding and the improvement was showing every week, culminating in Vic's first maximum on 1 September in the 47-31 win against Halifax. He was undoubtably the season's star. Thomsen had disappointed and Keith White dropped back a little, although he did win the London Riders Championship – denying Thomas a record-breaking third win by winning the run-off after both had scored. Petersen had done well in his first season and McNeil had been hampered by injury. Despite a late win at Birmingham, Hackney finishing bottom of the league. All of the riders were capable of being match-winners on occasion, but sadly very rarely together. Amazingly, they lost eight home league matches, five of them by just 2 points with a 38-40 scoreline.

1978 British League Record (19/19 teams)

Played	Won	Drawn	Lost	For	Against	Pts
36	10	1	25	1,264	1,538	21

1978 Cup Record

Round 1	King's Lynn	Won 97-57
Round 2	Exeter	Lost 54-102

1978 British League and Cup Averages (captain in italics)

Rider	Mts	Rds	Pts	BP	Total	CMA	Maxs
Finn Thomsen	30	135	246	14	260	7.71	1
Keith White	39	154	238	20	258	6.70	1
Barry Thomas	*40*	*176*	*246*	*42*	*288*	*6.55*	*1*
Vic Harding	39	163	223	33	256	6.28	1
Bo Petersen	34	142	190	28	218	6.14	
Bobby McNeil	27	91	100	20	120	5.28	
Ted Hubbard	15	55	63	9	72	5.24	
Malcolm Shakespeare	6	15	13	2	15	4.00	
Bent Rasmussen	10	34	24	7	31	3.65	
Billy Spiers	8	20	7	1	8	1.60	

[Laurie Etheridge 4.00 (5 matches only)]

1979 – Tragedy Again

Belief that the team was indeed better than the previous season's league position suggested was shown when Silver essentially tracked the same line-up that had commenced the 1978 season. The question was, could they all score to their full potential together? Completing the team was the seventeen-year-old Sean Willmott, filling the number seven position that had been so troublesome the year before. Willmott had started his career two years earlier at Weymouth, riding alongside Vic Harding. Silver had made further tentative enquiries again about Plech with his current Polish team, Gdansk, but was not happy enough with the initial responses to take the same gamble again and so Thomsen, Harding, McNeil, Petersen, White and Willmott lined up for the 1979 campaign, with the side again being led by Thomas. Thommo was celebrating ten years with Hackney and looking forward to a deserved testimonial, despite being just twenty-seven years old.

Hackney again struggled in their opening Gold Cup matches as well as being thrashed in their opening home league match, losing 29-49 to Swindon, and only managing a draw the following week against Sheffield. The riders were yet again performing inconsistently, but this was not the only reason behind Hackney's problems. Hackney was always regarded as a fair track with little home advantage. The steep banking always made the racing very exciting and Silver admitted during this difficult period that he had considered flattening it. Riders that were struggling came to The Wick and, finding the track such a dream to ride on, put in performances well above their CMA.

Keith White broke his ankle in the away defeat at Birmingham on 9 May, but even that bad luck could not be used as an excuse for what followed two nights later. A home thrashing against the only other London club was a disappointment too hard to hide, and the magnitude and manner of Wimbledon's 22-56 victory was too much for the victory-starved crowd. For the most part Silver's relationship with the Hackney crowd was always good, but for the first time Silver was booed by section of the support that had had enough. He admitted the following week that he was humiliated, degraded and ashamed and had deserved the stick the

Sean Willmott.

HACKNEY speedway rider Vic Harding, 27, was killed in a tragic crash at his home track last night.

Harding was flung from his machine into the safety fence after an accident involving Eastbourne rider Steve Weatherley.

The pair were racing along the straight almost locked together when the incident occurred. It was the last race of the British League Four Team tournament.

Harding was taken to Hackney Hospital and later transferred to Whipps Cross Hospital, where he died. Weatherley was also taken to hospital with serious back injuries.

Harding's girl friend and parents were all at the meeting, which was immediately abandoned.

Harding got his chance last night only because team-mate Bo Petersen had been injured in an earlier crash.

Hackney promoter Len Silver bought East-Ham born Harding from National League Weymouth in 1977. Harding, who lived in Canvey Island, Essex, earlier raced for Sunderland.

A national paper breaks the terrible news.

crowd had given him. He also admitted that he was still trying to obtain the services of Zenon Plech. Bo Petersen was scoring well, but two of the previous season's bright lights, Bobby McNeil and Vic Harding, were struggling with illness and engine problems respectively. In Harding's case, his average was almost three points down on the previous year, but he was trying hard to recapture his old form.

A new four-team tournament had been devised which saw three British League teams and one National League team competing over four meetings, one at each team's home track, with one rider from each team in each race. Unfortunately for Hackney, they were missing both Petersen and Thomsen for the first two legs at Canterbury and Eastbourne and it was no surprise that by the time the final leg was staged at The Wick, Hackney were 16 points behind the leaders Wimbledon. Friday 8 June 1979 was to be the blackest day in the history of Hackney Speedway. Ironically, this was also to be one of the best performances by Hackney of the season. From the start they set about the opposition, providing heat winner after heat winner as the deficit was slowing clawed back. Bo Petersen had won his first ride in heat 4, but had been injured after a bad heat 8 spill with Canterbury's Tim Hunt, which ruled both riders out of the meeting. This was the catalyst for the disaster to happen.

Bobby McNeil had blown his engine in his first ride and as his mechanics rushed to put a new engine in his bike, reserve Vic Harding found himself covering for both team-mates. By heat 11, Hackney had provided eight heat-winners and had closed the gap to just 3 points. The atmosphere was electric as the crowd sensed the chance for Hackney to complete an amazing comeback. Heat 12 saw Harding replace Petersen and finish second behind Eastbourne's reserve Steve Naylor, but Hackney hit back with victories from Thomas, Thomsen and McNeil, reappearing for his last ride. This left Hackney leading Eastbourne by 3 points with one race to go. The last heat saw Vic Harding again replacing the injured Petersen against Eastbourne's Steve Weatherly, Wimbledon's Roger Johns and Canterbury's veteran Nigel Boocock. Harding only needed 1 point to ensure Hackney's place in the final of the tournament and the crowd was full of expectation.

The tapes rose and for two laps the three British League riders fought a battle royal. The riders came round the pits bend to complete the second lap three abreast, Johns hugging the white line, Weatherly on the outside and Harding in the middle. As they raced across the start line Harding and Weatherly appeared to become locked together and were thrown into the fence, colliding with a lamp standard. The crash was so horrific an immediate hush fell over the crowd. It was obviously very serious. Harding was very quickly placed on a stretcher, his crash helmet still in place, and rushed from the circuit out through the pits and into the waiting ambulance. The meeting was immediately abandoned, fuelling the feeling of the gravity of the crash. Many Hackney fans would not leave the track, some staying until well after midnight, but when no news materialised people gradually went home.

The following morning, both the newspapers and the network of fans phoning each other revealed the full devastation of the incident. Harding had been killed, succumbing to his injuries during the night at Whipps Cross hospital, and Eastbourne's Weatherly had been paralysed. The supporters, the team and Len Silver were all devastated. Silver immediately withdrew the team from that night's away Knockout Cup clash with Halifax and cancelled the following week's meeting as a mark of respect. That Friday, Harding was cremated at the South Essex Crematorium in Upminster; he was the second Hackney rider to have been killed at Waterden Road.

Keith White: 'It was tragic. He was probably only in that meeting because I was injured at the time. The injury and that tragedy had a lot to do with why I didn't ride too well. In your subconscious you can't help thinking that it may not have happened had I been fit. It affects you more than you realise.'

Barry Thomas: 'He was a happy likeable bloke and he fitted in really well. Every rider is aware of how dangerous speedway is, but normally it's arms and legs and you don't get too many fatalities. I knew it was bad when he was being wheeled of the track. After the meeting we all went down the hospital and were told he was dead. It hit everyone very hard. It hit me hard.'

During the hiatus, and as difficult as it must have been, Silver had to turn his attention to a replacement. That replacement, two and a half years later than expected, was Zenon Plech. He finally made his first appearance for Hackney since 1976 in the final of the four-team tournament whose qualification had cost Hackney so dear. Having been used to Plech's non-appearance, this was made even more amazing since he was the only rider who had ridden in the previous night's World Pairs final in Vojens who made it back to Sheffield in time to appear.

The side continued the good form they had shown in the competition by winning their semi-final, aided by a Finn Thomsen maximum with Plech scoring 6. The final was ruined by rain and Hackney finished the tournament in fourth (and last) place, scoring just 8 points.

Plech made his home debut in the home match against Halifax on 29 June, but only scored a single point as another home defeat was added to the season's tally. Heavy away defeats at Coventry and Poole preceded home victories over Birmingham and Exeter, where Plech began to show the first signs of his world-class talent, twice beating Scott Autry in the latter match on his way to 9 points. His comeback to the world stage was completed on 20 July when Coventry hit town complete with World Champion Ole Olsen. There had been much hype that Plech was going to beat Olsen and he did so in true style, overtaking him from the back in heat 5 and smashing Olsen's track record on the way to a perfect 12-point maximum. Plech's influence on the team became obvious the following week when his absence, due to riding for Poland in the World Team Cup, left Hackney with another defeat following an emotional match with Eastbourne, which included the first staging of the Vic Harding Memorial Trophy.

Hackney received a much-needed boost when Thomsen qualified for the World Final, joining Plech in the final at Katowice. Hackney's away form was still disappointing, but at home when Plech was in the line-up, they looked a solid outfit. At last, the heat leaders were now performing consistently well with all three, Petersen, Thomsen and Plech, being unbeaten in the 10 August victory over Wolverhampton. The World Final provided Hackney with the biggest boost of the season, as Plech came within a whisker of being crowned World Champion, finishing as runner-up to the record-breaking Ivan Mauger, who was winning his sixth world title. Thomsen also showed his undoubted class, although engine problems in the final restricted his scoring to just 6 points.

Hackney's best chance of team success rested on a semi-final clash with King's Lynn in the inter-league Knockout Cup. In a close battle, Hackney succumbed 38-40 – being robbed when Lynn's Ian Turner fell after his footrest broke in heat 5, with the referee Graham Brodie excluding Plech. Ironically, the damage was really done by ex-Hawk Bent Rasmussen, who scored 7 points from reserve.

As his testimonial approached, the ever-popular Thomas did it again. 28 September brought the visit of Hull and, for the third time in consecutive years, Thomas beat World Champion Mauger – who must by this time have developed a complex about Thomas – this time in the opening heat. It was Mauger's only defeat and Hackney lost 33-45.

As the season entered its final phase, Bobby McNeil decided to retire. He had come to Hackney and immediately fitted in, proving to be very popular with the fans. He was scoring well, but several injuries and illness thwarted his scoring over the two seasons he spent at Hackney. It appeared that the accident to Harding had affected him badly and he had looked a shadow of his former self ever since.

Two more home defeats by Cradley and King's Lynn was enough to consign Hackney to finish in the wooden spoon position for the second consecutive year. Thomsen had delivered the goods, Plech had returned from the international wilderness and Bo Petersen had also continued his steady improvement. Willmott had performed well in a very difficult first year in the top flight, but White had experienced all kinds of misfortune and for him the year was a disaster: 'I broke my ankle early in the season at Birmingham. I was out for six weeks and when I came back the chain broke and I caught my foot between the safety fence and hurt the ankle again. Back then every single race in the British League was hard.'

Yet it was the tragic and devastating loss of Harding that 1979 will be remembered for, overshadowing Plech's achievements. And what of testimonial man Thomas? His season was disappointing and his average dropped by over a point, but he retained his place of affection with the Hackney crowd and remained capable of beating the best, winning the traditional Champions Chase only a week before his testimonial meeting – beating a line-up that included Plech, Thomsen and Gordon Kennett in the final.

Bobby McNeil.

1979 British League Record (18/18 teams)

Played	Won	Drawn	Lost	For	Against	Pts
34	9	1	24	1,130	1,515	19

1979 Cup Record

Round 1	Halifax	Conceded

1979 British League and Cup Averages (captain in italics)

Rider	Mts	Rds	Pts	BP	Total	CMA	Maxs
Zenon Plech	20	90	170	5	175	7.78	2
Bo Petersen	32	141	252	21	273	7.75	2
Finn Thomsen	32	135	244	16	260	7.71	5
Barry Thomas	*29*	*114*	*128*	*17*	*145*	*5.09*	
Vic Harding	9	36	34	5	39	4.33	
Bobby McNeil	26	80	67	13	80	4.00	
Sean Willmott	34	122	96	20	116	3.80	
Keith White	21	65	51	8	59	3.63	

[Also Ted Hubbard 2.93 (5 matches only)]

Vic Harding: A Tribute

Perhaps Vic Harding was destined to ride for Hackney, being a real East London lad; he was born in East Ham on 5 July 1952. Wisely, he always wanted to ensure he had a trade behind him and completed an apprenticeship to become a motor fitter. This led to a relatively late start in speedway, and it wasn't until the age of twenty-one that his career on shale really commenced.

Like many riders, he first rode a bike on waste ground at the age of seven and he became involved in scrambling before rapidly moving on to grass-track and joining the Kent Youth Motor Cycle Club. At the age of sixteen he took part in the same demonstration races at West Ham that had started Barry Thomas and Dave Jessup in their careers. He stayed with grass-track whilst his apprenticeship was completed, and kept looking for speedway opportunities by attending the Hackney training school – but these breaks were few and far between.

It was not until 1974 that George Barclay arranged for him to be included in a team selection race at Sunderland. He won the race and was in the Sunderland team. It was tough though, as Vic had to move the not inconsiderable distance to the North East and, in an indifferent season that saw him dropped and then recalled to the Sunderland team, he finished with a 3.71 CMA from 25 matches. During that season he had taken a liking to the Weymouth track when visiting with Sunderland and persuaded the promoter Harry Davies to give him a chance. With better machinery, he started to fulfil his potential and finished the 1975 season as Weymouth heat leader with a 6.82 CMA and he was elected captain for the following season, where he improved again to 7.18.

He was still at Weymouth in 1977 but, after a falling out with the promotion, he sought pastures new and, despite interest from King's Lynn, he was snapped up by Len Silver – who at this time still had an interest at Crayford – and Vic found himself doubling up between the Kent track and the Hawks. After only a few matches for Crayford, Silver severed his ties there and, as Vic was doing well in the British League, he was recalled to ride for the Hawks on a permanent basis.

The 1978 season dawned and Vic started out in the reserve berths, but by the end of the campaign he had become the Hawks' third heat leader with a creditable 6.46 and much was expected of him as the Hackney team lined up for 1979 – especially since Vic's bikes were being prepared by respected engine tuner Alex Macfadzean.

It was tough start and Vic struggled initially as he experimented with his new machinery. Ironically, he was returning to his best form and, on the fateful June night, he played an inspirational part in the Hawks' comeback. His death cast a shadow over Hackney. It profoundly touched everyone associated with the club and who were present that night. Like many others, he lost his life entertaining the public doing the thing he enjoyed most. Vic was never one of speedway's superstars, but was the type of rider that the sport could not exist without.

Vic Harding Memorial Trophy Winners

1979	Bo Petersen
1980	Bo Petersen
1981	Dave Jessup
1983	Finn Thomsen
1985	Martin Yeates
1988	Steve Schofield

The late Vic Harding in action.

4
THE WICK SPLUTTERS
1980-89

1980 – So Near And Yet II ...

'It is difficult to see the Hawks showing any dramatic improvement on last season's results' – thus read the *1980 Speedway Year Book* by Peter York. Berndt Odermatt, a little known German rider who had briefly appeared at Barry Thomas' testimonial the previous season, was the only newcomer to the side that finished bottom of the table in 1979, replacing Bobby McNeil.

As the season commenced, Hawks fans were feeling a sense of déjà vu as once again Zenon Plech failed to arrive. Hackney lost their opening four matches and Silver must have been dreading another year without the Polish star. However, by 11 April, Plech was back in England, although there was to be no immediate change in form as Hackney were thrashed 20-57 by King's Lynn. This time it was Silver who hit the roof:

Finn Thomsen inside Scott Autrey, and Steen Mastrup (hidden).

'Some frank words were spoken and all of the riders are now totally aware of my feelings and in particular that I, like all of you, am no longer prepared to tolerate the continual streams of problems that have beset the Hawks for the last three years. Keith must rapidly produce the goods and Bo and Zenon must always have two bikes available.'

It had been incredibly frustrating, with so many talented riders performing like champions one week and novices the next. The man to really suffer was Odermatt who, after just a handful of pretty poor performances, was dropped. The riot act had been read and Odermatt's replacement, Roman Jankowski, a young Pole recommended by Plech, was signed. These two events were about to change the whole season.

Jankowski looked like he could be the signing that Hackney needed and scored a very respectable 4 on his home debut against Reading on 18 April. Hackney still lost, however, and it was a further five days before the turning point. 23 April produced the shock of the season as Hackney won 40-38 at much-fancied Hull before another away win at Swindon, 46-32. Hull then returned to the Wick in the cup and took full revenge for the home league defeat. A disastrous night was later blamed on contaminated fuel, the Hawks also losing Willmott with a broken collarbone.

Thomsen and Plech were scoring well, but both were eclipsed by Petersen who was a revelation, scoring over 10 points per match. With Willmott, Jankowski, White and

Hackney, 1980. From left to right: Roman Jankowski, Keith White, Sean Willmott, Finn Thomsen, Bo Petersen, Zenon Plech, Len Silver. Barry Thomas is seated on the bike. A team destined not to improve!

Bo Petersen leads Peter Prinsloo.

Thomas giving solid backing, at last Hackney had an outfit that could challenge for the championship. Hackney were winning at home and added a further two away victories, at Leicester and Wimbledon. There was also a dubious rain-off at Belle Vue – who happened to be without the injured Peter Collins. 25 July posed the Hawks' biggest test of the season when the other team challenging for the championship, the Reading Racers, arrived at Waterden Road. Hackney were without Plech and Reading without Jiri Stancl (both riders being in action in the Continental Final). In their place were Les Collins and Kai Niemi. The match was electric from the outset, with the course of the championship hanging in the balance.

Hackney opened up a halfway 8-point lead, but with the help of tactical substitutes Reading clawed their way back. With two heats to go, only 2 points separated the sides. Thomsen masterfully won heat 12, beating Schwartz and Jan Andersson, and everything rested on heat 13. Thomsen led by example, his only defeat coming in the opening race, and Thomas unsurprisingly rose to the occasion. Petersen was still scoring phenomenally and, amazingly, had scored eight successive home league maximums. He lined up in the last heat with Collins against the in-form John Davies and ex-World Champion Barry Briggs' son, Tony. Petersen had been slightly reprimanded by Silver earlier in the season when, in a last-heat decider at Wimbledon, instead of sitting back in a match-winning position he rode hell for leather to win the race and complete his maximum. The tapes rose and Davies leapt into the lead with

A souvenir pencil drawing.

Collins and Petersen tucked in behind and this time, although the Hawks fans held their breath, there was no heroics and Hackney beat their rivals 40-38.

As August began, Hawks fans were celebrating again as both Zenon Plech and Finn Thomsen qualified for the World Championship final for the second season in succession. In Thomsen's case, he qualified after a fantastic performance at White City in the Intercontinental Final where he finished fifth on 10 points. After the meeting, Wimbledon's Larry Ross, who had been eliminated, protested that Thomsen's engine was oversized. The engine was measured and found perfectly legal.

Further away wins followed at Wolverhampton and Halifax, the latter match providing one of the greatest comebacks of all time. Hackney were trailing the Dukes after eight heats, 16-31, but rattled up four successive 5-1 results before sharing the last heat and winning the match 39-38. The victory was even more surprising since three riders, Willmott, Thomas and White, failed to score. Home and away victories over Eastbourne over the hot bank holiday weekend set up the Monday return match at Reading. On arriving at the track, Hackney were shocked to see gallons and gallons of water being dumped onto the circuit and, although it was hot and the home promotion wanted to ensure that the dust was kept down, the meeting started in fairly wet conditions and, struggling from the outset, Hackney were defeated for the first time in thirteen matches.

The World Final came and went, and with it Hackney's hopes of providing the World Champion – Thomsen with 7 points and Plech with 1 (who was beset with engine problems) represented a disappointing return after Plech's near miss the year before. The season's finale was always going to be tough for Hackney with the strong Cradley Heath and Coventry sides both visiting Waterden Road. Hackney faced Cradley on 3 October and another tense encounter followed with no more than 4 points separating the teams. Cradley, led by the impressive American Bruce Penhall and with the Dane Erik Gundersen also in the line-up, led by one point after heat 6, Hackney drew ahead by 1 point in heat 9 and the gap remained the same until the heat 11 clash of the unbeaten giants –Petersen versus Penhall.

Penhall drew first blood, and with Alan Grahame in third giving Cradley a 2-4, Cradley moved 1 point in front. A shared heat in heat 12 set up another heart-stopping, last-heat decider and rematch between the big two. Hackney now desperately needed a heat advantage to ensure another win. Penhall again led from the start, with Petersen desperately chasing in second. As they came round the pits bend to complete the second lap, Petersen made a mighty effort to pass Penhall but overcooked it and fell. It was all over. Penhall won the re-run, Cradley the match 37-40 and with it Hackney's hopes of winning the British League disappeared. The impetus was gone. Hackney closed with a double-header victory over Coventry and King's Lynn and a home London Cup victory over Wimbledon, but this was not sufficient to win the trophy.

A season that started so miserably had turned into one of the most exciting, despite finishing with no silverware whatsoever. With effectively the same team that had finished bottom of the table twelve months earlier, Hackney had finished as runners-up in the British League to Reading, just 3 points adrift of the championship, and had provided exciting opposition almost everywhere they went.

Zenon Plech and Finn Thomsen were undoubtedly world-class riders who, on their day, were as good as anyone. Thomsen also joined the illustrious list of London Riders champions. Bo Petersen had been magnificent, topping the league averages for most of the season before slipping to fourth place behind Peter Collins, Hans Nielsen and Dave Jessup. He also finished the season as holder of the prestigious Golden Helmet Match Race Championship after beating Chris Morton – which included one terrific scrap in the Hackney leg that resulted in a dead heat. He scored 4 in the BLRC. Roman Jankowski was one of the finds of the season: popular and exciting, he scored well in his debut campaign. Sean Willmott improved his average by a couple of points and Barry Thomas – although his scoring had becoming possibly more erratic – was the same old Thommo. With the Cinderella tag finally cast off, Hackney would surely march on to greater glories.

1980 British League Record (2/17 teams)

Played	Won	Drawn	Lost	For	Against	Pts
32	23	0	9	1,300	1,188	46

1980 Cup Record

Round 1		Hull		Lost 86-130

1980 British League and Cup Averages (captain in italics)

Rider	Mts	Rds	Pts	BP	Total	CMA	Maxs
Bo Petersen	34	148	365	15	380	10.27	12
Zenon Plech	24	101	189	16	205	8.12	3
Finn Thomsen	32	135	244	18	262	7.76	2
Sean Willmott	29	105	122	22	144	5.49	
Barry Thomas	*34*	*121*	*137*	*23*	*160*	*5.29*	
Roman Jankowski	32	118	126	27	153	5.19	1
Keith White	33	98	106	15	121	4.94	1
Kevin Smith	6	24	17	5	22	3.67	

1981 – Anti-Climax

Perhaps one would have thought that Hackney may have fielded an unchanged line-up in their bid to go just one better. The bolt out of the blue was from skipper Barry Thomas. Fed up with struggling in the British League, he requested a move to Crayford in the hope that this would revitalise his career, Silver could not talk him out of it. Thomas became Hackney's back-up man and his replacement was traditional number eight Ted Hubbard, who was back for another spell at the Wick mounted on one of Bo Petersen's 1980 machines.

Finn Thomsen was the new captain and it was obvious that he was going to take the role very seriously. Plech, Petersen and Willmott were back too, but Keith White was transferred: 'Len wanted me to ride at Rye House but I was a bit unhappy because I thought he would leave me out of the Hackney team and keep Roman (Jankowski) who was good, but I would have been there all year and he was absent a lot. I wanted to stay in the best league. So I went to Coventry.' His replacement was Rye House star Bob Garrad. Garrad had been making his mark the previous season on loan to Leicester, but Silver had managed to persuade him to join parent club Hackney instead of switching to the Midlands track as was expected. There was Pole trouble again, although this time with Jankowski, and Hackney started the season without his services whilst his Polish club, Unia Leszno, decided if he could ride in England.

New to the 1981 season was the League Cup competition, with British League teams split into two groups with the winners meeting in the final and the matches extended to 16 heats. 8 May brought Hackney's first home defeat at the hands of Swindon and this prompted Silver to strengthen the side. When Leszno gave a final no to Jankowski being released, he then moved swiftly to sign fellow Pole Andrzej Huszcza from Leicester.

But two weeks later he still had not arrived and, although Hackney defeated Poole, they lost Hubbard with a dislocated shoulder and Garrad with concussion. Coventry were the visitors on 29 May in the cup. Huszcza made his debut but failed to score and Hackney were soundly beaten, 37-59. It was, however, the events of heat 8 that had everybody talking. Petersen led Ole Olsen but on turn two Olsen, on the inside, moved out towards Petersen, did not stop coming and took him straight into the safety fence. Olsen was immediately excluded, but Petersen was incensed and ran the length of the track back to the pits entrance to confront his fellow countryman and he had to be restrained. Hackney exited the Knockout Cup the following night 33-63, with Huszcza scoring 11 points.

Hackney finished sixth in their League Cup group, with only Eastbourne and Wimbledon below them. In addition, they were out of the Knockout Cup, had lost all their away matches and one of their Polish riders was missing – a familiar story for Hawks fans. Bob Garrad was struggling and Zenon Plech was having a poor season by his own high standards and found himself at reserve, as Hackney's home league campaign got underway against Swindon on 5 June. Barry Thomas was back as the other reserve, replacing Hubbard and putting in some impressive displays. Yet even with this advantage the match was lost 38-40. The enigmatic Huszcza failed to score.

Andy Huszcza.

For the first time in Hackney's history, they staged a test match against Denmark on 12 June. Thomsen and Tommy Knudsen provided token resistance, but England (again under the leadership of Silver) won easily 62-46, Petersen scoring a disappointing 6. Away defeats at Hull and Leicester followed, but Hackney did manage to sign Ian Clark from the Lions in a bid to strengthen the team at the expense of Garrad, who was loaned back to Rye House. A full-time replacement for the injured Hubbard was also signed – Roman Jankowski. Jankowski scored 5 at Poole on his first performance in 1981 and Hackney emerged victorious 41- 37, their first away win of the year. Any hopes of the tide turning were extinguished when the Danish Motor Union suspended Bo Petersen from riding for fourteen days for arriving late for Intercontinental Final practice. This practice session did not require compulsory attendance and there were rumours that Olsen had used his influence to pay back the earlier incident.

Hackney would have to use guests, but that was a disaster from the start. Malcolm Simmons failed to score at King's Lynn and Hackney lost by just 6 points. Worse was to come during the home match on 14 August against Cradley. Hackney were keen to avenge the previous season's costly home defeat and dent the Heathen's championship challenge. Petersen's guest was former Heathen Bobby Schwartz, best friend of Cradley number one Bruce Penhall. Perhaps this was not an astute move on the part of Silver – who obviously felt that Schwartz, as a professional rider, would put feelings aside and do his best. In the end, Hackney rode their heart out. Plech was back to his superb best with 10 and Barry Thomas chipped in with 7, but it was not enough as Hackney succumbed in the last heat, 38-40. Schwartz only scored 3 and with the score 34-32 he trailed round at the back in the vital heat 12.

Roman Jankowski.

Bo Petersen.

Hackney had hardly tracked the same side twice, international call-ups taking their toll on a team with three Poles and two Danes. But a glimpse of what may have been was seen on 28 August when the Hawks tracked (for the first time that season) their strongest possible line-up: Thomsen, Petersen, Plech, Jankowski, Huszcza, Willmott and Thomas. The result was that Hull, complete with Ivan Mauger, were soundly beaten 55-23. Riding for Crayford had breathed new life into Thomas and many fans were calling for him to be back in the Hawks line-up. Silver responded: 'Both he (Thomas) and I agree that his better performances are in evidence because he is racing successfully for Crayford and that the probability is that if he came back full time he'd quickly relapse into the slow-gating, low-scoring Barry that we all remember.' It would not stop calls for Thomas' return, and 7 points in the home win that week against King's Lynn did nothing to deter the Hackney faithful.

As the season drew to a close, Silver was already announcing signings for the new season. Jankowski and Huszca were both extremely popular with the Hackney public but had not scored consistently. To ensure a work permit for the following season they had to finish with a CMA above 6.00 and it was becoming increasing obvious that neither would make the cut-off. Grass-track rider Martin Hagon was already signed for the new season and Bo Petersen had recommended another young Dane, Jens Rasmussen (no relation to Bent), who was also signed after a couple of impressive second-half performances.

Hackney defeated Reading on 2 October and Schwartz cleared the air with Silver, admitting that he was emotionally confused during the Cradley match. Another home win followed the next week against Coventry, but a broken foot sustained by Jankowski effectively ended any hope of him reaching the target average and on 16 October Huszcza scored 7 against his old club – although it was not enough to prevent Leicester winning 38-40 or to elevate the Pole above the minimum target.

Wimbledon completed an aggregate London Cup victory and Hackney finished in a disappointing eighth place in the British League. Petersen had ridden well again, although his scoring was down on the previous year. He lost the Golden Helmet in his first defence to Michael Lee and missed out on the World Final again. Finn Thomsen had scored well again but more importantly had become a superb skipper, leading the way not just on track but off it too. Plech had shown some of his old brilliance but had lost the third heat leader spot to the impressive Sean Willmott, who had ridden quietly but effectively for most of the season and had raised his average by over 2 points. Jankowski and Huszcza had suffered from the late start and inevitable commuting.

Clark and Garrad had both disappointed and Hubbard again had his senior league career disrupted by injuries and machine troubles: 'Len sorted me out with Bo's bike and it was very quick at the beginning but the engine went off and I had to have it done up. It was never the same again and then my shoulder was dislocated, it went out and then back in again – it hurt.' Barry Thomas had shown glimpses of the old Thomas and had been superb stand-in when required, as well as scoring a 9.10 average for Crayford. In the end, although not a disaster, the season certainly was an anti-climax.

1981 British League Record (8/16 teams)

Played	Won	Drawn	Lost	For	Against	Pts
30	12	2	16	1,182	1,157	26

1981 Cup Record

Round 1	Coventry	Lost 70-122

1981 British League, League Cup and Cup Averages (captain in italics)

Rider	Mts	Rds	Pts	BP	Total	CMA	Maxs
Bo Petersen	42	205	477	14	491	9.58	4
Finn Thomsen	*41*	*189*	*347*	*23*	*370*	*7.83*	
Sean Willmott	46	216	345	35	380	7.04	
Zenon Plech	39	163	224	32	256	6.28	
Barry Thomas	20	79	88	21	109	5.52	
Roman Jankowski	19	67	72	15	87	5.19	
Bob Garrad	31	134	145½	20	165½	4.94	
Andrzej Huszcza	13	49	42	10	52	4.25	
Ted Hubbard	19	57	43	8	51	3.58	
Ian Clark	9	23	12	6	18	3.13	
Simon Aindow	13	34	9	0	9	1.06	

HACKNEY HERO

ZENON PLECH

Darling of the Hackney Crowd

Zenon Plech was born in the Polish town of Zwierzyn on 1 January 1953 and he first rode a speedway bike during practice sessions at the local Stal Gorzow track in 1969. He soon made the Gorzow team and in 1971 won his first trophy, the Polish Silver Helmet. He recalls: 'We spent all the money we earned from points but it is different now, there was no big money, especially in Poland. In past years when you tried to be a good rider there was nothing to learn in the Polish league but now with riders from USA, Australia, Swedish and England all riding in Poland it is as good as the British League. I started when I was sixteen and for me speedway was everything. I always tried to do my best but I didn't always get the luck.'

1972 saw Zenon win the Polish National Championship for the first time and he also represented Poland in the World Team Cup in Germany, where he scored 7 points to help his home country to third place. 1973 was the year he first broke onto the international stage. He finished third in the World Pairs final, partnering Zbigniew Marcinkowski and scoring 14 points, and again represented Poland in the World Team Cup, scoring 5 of Poland's paltry total of 8 at Wembley. That year Zenon rode in his first World Final, finishing in third place with 12 points. This superb performance was overshadowed though by a shock winner, fellow countryman Jerzy Szczakiel, who beat Ivan Mauger after the legendary New Zealander fell in the run-off.

Disappointingly, Zenon was only one point short of making that run-off himself. He lined up for his final heat requiring a win to join Mauger and Szczakiel, against Peter Collins and Russians Grigori Chlynovski and Valeri Gordeev. Chlynovski also had 10 points and also needed a win to make the run-off. Collins led from the tapes with Plech second, but they collided on the first lap and both the Russians managed to get past Collins. There was confusion as to whether the race had been stopped at this stage but not before Chlynovski had tried to overtake Plech, causing him to fall. After a 30-minute delay and countless arguments, it was decided to exclude Chlynovski but award the race in the order prevalent when Collins and Plech collided. Zenon's chance was gone and he had to be content with third place.

1973 was also the year that Zenon rode at Hackney for the first time. England took on Poland in the *Daily Mirror* World League and, on a night when rain ensured appalling conditions, Zenon scored 11 paid 12 from 4 rides and fell in the other one. Len Silver had taken notice: 'I had been a few times in England with Test matches against England. At Hackney it was heavy rain and all mud but we raced because of the television. I just enjoyed racing. When I first came to England we racing for bicycle money. I still remember £2.40 per start and £3.60 per point. The Hackney track is the best. You can race everywhere and the banking was excellent.'

1974 saw Zenon win the Polish National Championship and he again qualified for the World Final. This time though he could only score 8 points at Gothenberg to finish in joint seventh place. Poland were to have an even worse World Team Cup, for although they scored 5 more points than the previous year, the fact that the meeting was held at Katowice made the result a major embarrassment. Zenon scored 4 points.

Poland's poor form continued in the 1975 World Team Cup, finishing last in Norden with 9 points, Zenon failing to score. Len Silver had miraculously managed to obtain permission for him to sign for Hackney and after the meeting he returned to England in the boot of Len's car! 'You know, my English was not so good. I am sitting beside Len, but I have no documents only my passport. He took me from Norden after the World Team Cup and we drive to England by crossing from Ostend to Dover, we were just lucky. I was young and not thinking about what could happen. When my Polish bosses tell me I am going to ride for Hackney and for Len Silver I was pleased.'

Zenon was to become one of the most popular riders to ride for Hackney over the coming seasons, as well as one of the most spectacular. His debut season saw him finish with a credible 7-point average (although from only 4 matches), but another

Zenon Plech.

disappointing World Final at Wembley saw him score 4 points to finish in joint twelfth place. Zenon built upon his first season's experience and continued in good form for the Hawks in 1976, even though his average remained much the same.

The World Team Cup was held at White City and England had been unexpectedly knocked out during the qualifying stages. Poland came close to victory, finishing in second place behind Australia just 3 points adrift. Zenon scored 6 points and, but for a nasty collision with the White City safety fence, may have become World Team Champion.

1977 arrived, but Zenon didn't. 'I was very upset. I say to myself I must go to England again and I change club because the new club say I can go to England again but I have to go to the Army first. I was ready to go and I know where I want to go but…' Arguments aside, what followed was an even more sensational story. Zenon was riding in a qualifier for the 1978 World Championship in May of that year and had moved forward to the next round. It was a miserable cold and wet meeting and Zenon was feeling very unwell. He returned to Poland and went to his local hospital. The doctors diagnosed heart disease and told Zenon his sporting career was over. He spent over ten weeks in hospital recovering, but the recuperative period breathed new life into his career. 'I go to the World Championship and am qualifying to the next round but I felt so terrible. I go back to Gdansk and my doctors say you are very, very ill. I lay down on the bed for two weeks and don't move. He said I had a heart problem and that I have no more chance for speedway. But I told him my life is speedway and I started racing again.'

He returned to Hackney in 1979 and became Polish National Champion for the third time. He was riding better than ever and that season culminated in a return to the World Final rostrum, finishing in second place and coming within a whisker of becoming World Champion. Was Zenon robbed? He is typically modest: 'I am in a race with Kelly Moran. I raced too gently, I think. If I had pushed a little harder I may have been level on points with Mauger.' Zenon again rode in the World Team Cup that season when the final returned to White City. Poland finished third with Zenon scoring 4 points.

Zenon returned to Hackney in 1980 and helped the Hawks to second place in the league, finishing with his highest British League CMA, scoring over 8 points per match for the first time. He won the Continental Championship on his way to the World Final and again rode in the World Team final. Held in Poland, another poor performance saw the home nation finish in third place with 15, Zenon scoring 5.

1981 was to be Zenon's last season in Hackney colours. When the Polish authorities started to cast doubt again on his availability, Len Silver finally ran out of patience and sought a replacement. Plech turned out briefly for Sheffield later in 1982 but it was not a success and his British career finally came to an end.

What about his team-mates? 'I remember from the beginning everyone. I remember at first the pairs meeting they used to call the Bonanza Pairs Championship and I won the meeting with Steve Lomas. I remember Broady [Mike Broadbanks], Trevor Hedge, Laurie Etheridge and Dave Morton and Crockett [Dave

Kennett]. I was very great friends with all of them. And Ted Hubbard and Thommo. I had a very good time with Thommo over a long time. We drove to a meeting in Germany and on the way back I was asleep on the front seat and Thommo was driving but the petrol ran out. We stop on the German motorway and Thommo was putting petrol in the tank and a big lorry hit us. When Thommo saw the lorry he jumped the barrier. The truck hit us and the car went 50 yards. The bikes and car were completely damaged and Thommo thought he had killed me! I think he thought he would just dig a big hole on the motorway. I just woke up and everything was okay. Finn Thomsen was a very good friend: he always did my engines before the World Final. Bo Petersen too. We had a very good time at Hackney; there was a big public and after the meeting we all went upstairs to the pub and give autographs. Nowadays riders are so busy and have no time for the fans. After the meeting they go home – different world, manic. We should do things for the fans.'

There is no doubt that Zenon was much better than his British League averages would suggest. The political climate in Poland and poor standard of living no doubt had an adverse affect on his career. Poor machinery and unreasonably being prevented from riding every week against the world's best riders hardly helped and one wonders what may have been achieved had he been given the support of his countrymen that riders like Tomasz Gollob enjoy today. Zenon is modest again on the subject: 'I think in the past we still had good mechanics. Trevor Hedge and Alex McFadzean, he was very good to Vic Harding and then me.' When asked about being adopted by Len Silver he laughs and says 'I remember that, yeah. I was young enough but you know...' As if proof was necessary that Zenon is such a nice guy, he says 'Please print my best wishes to everyone who supported me at Hackney and also to my friends at Wimbledon and White City.'

1982 – Heartache Again

The will he/won't he saga with Plech was not even given any chance to unfold with its usual dramas. His club demanded that Plech return home seventeen times during the season. Silver had learnt his lesson, said no to the popular Pole and signed Australian John Titman. Born on 26 January 1951, Titman was an experienced campaigner who had ridden for Halifax, Exeter and, for the last four seasons, Leicester. He qualified for two World Finals, in 1978 (scoring 7) and 1979 (scoring 6) and came to The Wick with a 7.44 CMA. Unfortunately Titman like Plech, the man he replaced, failed to start the season owing to other racing commitments. Another major signing was the Czech Toni Kasper, joining Martin Hagon and Jens Rasmussen. A new-look Hawks team took to the track with only Petersen, Thomsen and Willmott retained.

Without Titman, Hackney lost their opener, a 'Revenge Challenge' match against Cradley 32-46. But twenty-fours hours later opened their League Cup campaign with a win at Swindon, 41-37. 22 April saw Hackney visit their bogey side, Ipswich. Over many years Ipswich had been a thorn in Hackney's side especially during some of the old

John Titman.

home and away Good Friday clashes. To make matters worse, the Ipswich promoter John Berry was not liked by the Hackney crowd and did not get on well with Silver. The crux of the problems in the main was the bumpy state of the Ipswich track, which in addition always seemed to be over-watered like a ploughed field, making for many taunts from the Hackney fans when visiting Foxhall Heath. The 24-54 drubbing Hackney experienced led Silver to finally vent his views about Ipswich in the programme notes for the home match against Eastbourne on 30 April.

'We visited Ipswich eight days ago and met with disaster – not for the first time, I might add. While I was there I pondered the reason for our poor performances at the East Anglian track and realised that there is a carefully orchestrated system of operation there, cleverly designed to undermine the chances of opposing sides. To start with an already disproportionate track (its straights are too long for its tight bends) is made more difficult to negotiate by very patchy depths of shale in the corners, rendering it quite alarming for the first seven or eight races until the shale gets thrown to the outside. But that isn't all. What seems deliberately, various officials tend to undermine the confidence of some riders (presumably only the visitors) by 'nit picking' about machinery or even just standing over them while they do things like changing gears as a constant and harassing reminder that haste is required, but in the process making the riders feel uneasy.'

John Titman finally made his home debut that night against the Eagles, after a workshop injury to his finger had added even more delays to his first appearance. He failed to score and another home defeat, 36-42, was the result. The League Cup came to an end with the home match against Ipswich on 4 June. Silver must have really psyched the riders up as a real team effort saw the Hawks home 42-35. Thomsen and Willmott clinched the match in heat 12 with a 5-0 win. The bad feeling between the two teams led the Hackney crowd to sing the 'Laurel and Hardy' theme when Berry walked along the Hackney track with Thomsen making uncomplimentary gestures behind his back!

Hackney finished their League Cup group in fifth place, having won only once away and having lost twice at home. Rasmussen and Kasper were scoring well, providing a small amount of comfort, but Willmott was failing to live up to the promise he had shown a year earlier. Hackney managed a draw at Poole and a shock victory over Ipswich the following night, but while the Hawks were on a roll, one of the wettest

Junes on record wiped out all but their away fixture at Belle Vue, where they were soundly beaten 25-53.

9 July saw Cradley back in town and Hackney were desperate to avenge the defeats from 1980 and 1981. More controversy was to follow though, when Bruce Penhall flew back to the USA to aid a sick relative and missed the match – although many blamed his absence on the crowd reaction he received, having openly helped his American team-mates in the Overseas Final five days previous. Cradley had applied for a guest but had been turned down and a weakened team was beaten 42-36. Cradley protested. The following week Reading was the visitors, which saw the return of Schwartz and another black chapter in Hackney's history was about to written.

Rye House stars Marvyn Cox and Bob Garrad had been drafted in as replacement for Sean Willmott and Toni Kasper. The match had been finely balanced at 18-18 after six

Toni Kasper.

heats but Reading moved ahead with a 1-5 in heat 7 and a 2-4 in heat 8, with much of the damage being done by American Denny Pyeatt, Schwartz's protégé. Heat 9 saw Petersen and Cox pitted against Pyeatt and the third American in the Reading team, Steve Gresham. Petersen led easily from the tapes, but Pyeatt and Cox were tussling for second and third place. On the pits bend Cox and Pyeatt collided, Pyeatt, after straightening up seemingly pulling the throttle back and shot straight into the fence at full speed, hitting the lamp standard beyond. Yet again it was clear that the accident had been a bad one. The match was immediately abandoned. Cox had broken his wrist and Pyeatt was rushed to Hackney Hospital, where he succumbed to his injuries the following morning. Understandably, Silver was devastated that another fatality had occurred at the Wick: 'The shocking events of last week's tragic accident have left me feeling twenty years older and totally shattered'.

Many unsavoury words were spilled in the press by some of the American contingent regarding the Hackney track. No doubt they were very upset at the what had happened to their fellow countryman, but Hackney was not the only track to have old-fashioned lamp standards outside the safety fence and many felt that the accident record was more to do with riders overriding the banked track. Hackney staged the final test match against Denmark on 6 August after the original fixture was rained off. Petersen scored 8 and Thomsen 7 as Denmark won 40-68, although England won the series 2-1.

More bad news followed though as Hackney lost the services of Toni Kasper for the rest of the season after he dislocated his hip and fractured his pelvis whilst riding as a guest for Reading on 13 September. Hackney was to use rider replacement for him and back to the team as number eight came Barry Thomas. Hackney secured a double-header victory over Halifax 49-29 and Sheffield 47-31. The second match was like a Hackney reunion as Dave Morton and Zenon Plech returned. Plech showed some of his old style, scoring 6, but Morton could only manage four. Both were eclipsed by a vintage display from Thomas, who scored 6 and 7 – the highlight of which was a superb outside pass of Morton.

A fortnight later came another double header and Thomas performed even better. He scored 8 in the victory over Ipswich but saved his best performance for the second match, scoring 6 including beating another World Champion Ole Olsen, although this was not sufficient to prevent a 34-43 defeat. The Hawks badly missed Petersen, who was forced to withdraw after sustaining concussion after a first-ride fall. Twenty-four hours later and the news was even worse. An X-ray had revealed that Petersen had broken his ankle. He did not ride again that season. Hackney were now without their top two and it showed as they lost at home to Birmingham 36-41, with Thomas top-scoring again with a superb 10 points. Speculation started again about Thomas signing full time again, but he was enjoying life in the National League and it seemed he would not return to Hackney on a permanent basis.

Another bout of rain brought the season to a sudden and dismal end. Amazingly, Cradley won their appeal lodged earlier in the season and the match had to be replayed – ironically in a double header with Reading. Two victories at least ended the season on a happy note for Hackney, beating Reading 42-36 and Cradley (who were now permanently without Penhall, who had retired following his second World Championship win) 40-38.

Kasper had been the find of the season, but sadly his campaign had been cut short by injury. Titman had fitted in nicely as second string and Rasmussen had scored well in his first season. Petersen's scoring was down again and Thomsen had slipped to fifth place in the averages, but not before scoring 5 in the BLRC. Willmott was very disappointing, his CMA was down by over 2 points per match and Hagon had struggled in his debut season. Hackney had finished a respectable seventh in the league, but it could have been better considering how well Kasper and Titman had ridden.

1982 British League Record (7/15 teams)

Played	Won	Drawn	Lost	For	Against	Pts
28	12	3	13	1,058½	1,121½	27

1982 Cup Record

Round 1	Halifax	Lost 71-85

1982 British League, League Cup and Cup Averages (captain in italics)

Rider	Mts	Rds	Pts	BP	Total	CMA	Maxs
Bo Petersen	37	162	365	15	380	9.38	3
Barry Thomas	6	22	40	6	46	8.36	
Finn Thomsen	*41*	*167*	*282½*	*22*	*304½*	*7.29*	*2*
John Titman	36	145	215	24	239	6.59	
Toni Kasper	31	120	181	15	196	6.53	
Sean Willmott	40	169	204	48	252	5.96	
Jens Rasmussen	44	162	191	33	224	5.53	
Bob Garrad	10	31	26	5	31	4.00	
Martin Hagon	43	124	90	19	109	3.52	

1983 – Silver Clouds Over

Dark clouds were gathering over speedway. Wembley was lost as a venue and crowds were falling. In addition, there would be no World Champion in the British League following Penhall's retirement. Hackney started the new season with a completely unchanged line-up. The rain that washed out the last month of the previous year was still prevalent as the 1983 season commenced. Hackney's first two home matches fell victim to the weather. Without the opportunity for a morale-boosting home fixture, perhaps it was not surprising that the three away matches that took place resulted in comfortable wins for the home teams – Swindon, Poole and Wimbledon.

Bo Petersen appeared fully recovered from his broken leg, top-scoring with 17 at Swindon. The Wimbledon match was held in atrocious conditions and only Barry Thomas looked comfortable on his way to scoring 8 points. Thommo was replacing Toni Kasper.

The home campaign finally got underway and Swindon were beaten at the Wick. The double was completed over Ipswich and there was an away win at Eastbourne on 24 April. Five days later, with King's Lynn the visitors at Waterden Road, it all turned to disaster. The Hawks were sitting nicely 8 points ahead after heat 7, but in heat 8 taking a rider replacement ride for the still absent Kasper, Petersen fell and broke his leg. The Hawks managed to stay in front and win the match 41-36. The League Cup campaign was completed using guests and the remainder of the away League Cup matches were lost. At home Hackney lost to Wimbledon 33-45 in the first match of a double header on 20 May. Bob Garrad was listed as number eight but did not ride.

In the second match, Thomas was number eight and rode in three races scoring 7 points: Hackney ran out easy victors over Poole, 48-30. Hackney missed out on the League Cup final finishing second in their group, 6 points adrift of Wimbledon, who also won the held-over staging of the 1982 London Cup.

The British League campaign commenced at Belle Vue on 18 June with the Hawks lining up at full strength for the first time that season following the return of both Petersen and Kasper. They were soundly beaten 31-46 and Petersen, who had returned too early, was back on the sidelines. With Kasper missing much of the time riding back in Czechoslovakia, it was back to guests and rider replacement again. For the third successive season Hackney staged a test match against Denmark. This time the match was the deciding third test and England won 65-43 with Thomsen scoring 6.

Hackney returned to full strength again as Reading hit town on 15 July. The night's temperature was very warm and the track was watered approximately 15 minutes before the start of the first race. This left the surface a little tricky for the first couple of races and heat 4 saw Jens Rasmussen and Reading's Jan Andersson collide, with Rasmussen taking no further part in the meeting. The bad feeling between Schwartz and Hackney boiled violently to the surface again. Schwartz ran an uncomfortable last in heat 3 and, following the heat 4 crash, he completely lost his cool, shouting and gesticulating at Silver. Schwartz never wanted to ride in the fixture in the first place and after his outpouring of emotion he walked out of the rest of the meeting, which Hackney won 43-35. Hackney's history was steeped in poor away form and inconsistent

Jens Rasmussen.

performances and this season was no different. In the main, all the riders were scoring consistently well but not scoring well together.

As September commenced a bombshell was dropped. In his programme notes on 9 September, Silver revealed that a new consortium would run Hackney Speedway from the start of the following season led by Chris Shears, with Malcolm Simmons re-signing for the Hawks as rider/manager. By 7 October, Silver was announcing that Shears' application for a licence had been approved and the future of the Hawks was secured. The London Cup was lost for the second time in a season, despite beating Wimbledon 41-37, and suddenly it was the last night of the season; Silver's last meeting in charge after twenty years was the Vic Harding Memorial trophy.

An all-star line-up, which included Thomas and Plech, was assembled to bid farewell to Silver and pay tribute to Harding's memory. Silver had worked hard to turn Hackney into a successful club and although on-track success had been scarce, Hackney had survived thanks to his efforts. Finn Thomsen rode to an immaculate 15-point maximum and was the night's eventual victor. Thomsen was back to his best in his sixth season, in which time he had become one of the classiest performers ever to ride for Hackney. He became World Team Champion for the third time following wins in 1978 and 1981. Bo Petersen was hit hard by injuries and his average suffered accordingly. The high spot was victory in the London Riders Championship and he also scored 8 in the BLRC. Jens Rasmussen rode well, improving into the third heat leader spot, and John Titman

Hackney, 1983. From left to right: Len Silver, Toni Kasper, Martin Hagon, Jens Rasmussen, Bo Petersen, Sean Willmott, John Titman. Finn Thomsen is seated on the bike.

Finn Thomsen works on his machinery, reputed to be amongst the fastest in the world.

continued as a reliable second string. Willmott was again disappointing and he finished the season with a broken arm; Hagon did not fare much better. The biggest disappointment was Toni Kasper. No doubt his late return plus numerous Continental commitments took their toll and his scoring was 3 points a match down. One wonders what Kasper and Plech before him may have achieved if their home countries had done more to encourage their careers.

Hackney finished in seventh place in the British League for the second consecutive campaign and the new season beckoned with new management – but the drama was far from over.

1983 British League Record (7/15 teams)

Played	Won	Drawn	Lost	For	Against	Pts
28	14	0	14	1,072	1,106	28

1983 Cup Record

Round 1	Cradley	Lost 67-89

1983 British League, League Cup and Cup Averages (captain in italics)

Rider	Mts	Rds	Pts	BP	Total	CMA	Maxs
Bo Petersen	30	128	254	17	271	8.47	
Finn Thomsen	*42*	*189*	*340*	*35*	*375*	*7.94*	*2*
Barry Thomas	6	13	18	6	24	7.39	
Jens Rasmussen	43	162	239	34	273	6.74	
Sean Willmott	43	191	252	49	301	6.30	2
John Titman	41	167	233	28	261	6.25	
Martin Hagon	44	125	131	20	151	4.83	1
Toni Kasper	18	62	61	7	68	4.39	
Bob Garrad	12	27	21	8	9	4.30	

HACKNEY HERO

LEN SILVER

The Best Since Hoskins?

Showman or troublemaker? One thing is certain and that is that Len is passionate about speedway. Len was born on 2 February 1932 and lived close to Hackney Stadium in nearby Bow. His was educated firstly at Lauriston Road School, Hackney before moving to Stratford Grammar. He left school at sixteen and commenced work as an office boy for a publishing company in Holborn.

After the war, Len became a keen speedway fan supporting local team, West Ham, and in particular the Australian rider Aub Lawson. Between 1946 and 1950 he rode for the Stratford Hammers cycle speedway team: Dennis Day and Jimmy Heard, both latterly destined to become Hawks, were amongst his team-mates.

National Service called in 1950 and Len was conscripted to the Royal Air Force, where he spent two years – including a spell in Egypt as a dispatch rider. Following his demobilsation at the end of 1952, Len decided that he wanted a more prominent role in speedway racing and attended the Rye House training school, where he impressed enough to earn a second-half booking at West Ham. He continued practising during that winter at Rayleigh and – somewhat ironically in view of the rivalry which was to later build up between the two clubs – Len signed for Ipswich, where he spent five seasons before a broken arm sustained at Southampton brought his career to what turned out to be a temporary end.

After the accident, Len started his own car sales business at Maryland Point in Stratford, but he returned to track action in 1960 when the then Ipswich promoter Vic Gooden tempted him back to Ipswich. His second term at Ipswich did not last very long and the following year he was transferred to Exeter in what to be his most successful period. He was made the Exeter skipper in 1962 and, during the course of the year, made ten successful defences of the Silver Sash Match Race Championship. To cap it all, he won that season's Provincial League Rider Championship at Belle Vue, beating Wayne Briggs, Brian Craven and Guy Allott in the winner-take-all final. This victory was undoubtedly the highlight of his riding career.

In 1963, Len started to consider a possible future in promoting. 'I was still riding for Exeter and I heard about a greyhound stadium at Charlton that had gone out of use and I fancied becoming a promoter so I made approaches to the owners of the stadium, which was a company called London Stadiums Ltd, to rent the stadium for speedway. I met with quite good response and I felt negotiations were going reasonably well. I was riding for Exeter at Newport and Mike Parker who was a fairly big promoter in those days, he promoted at various tracks came up to me and said "I understand you're negotiating for Charlton stadium"; well I was gob-smacked that he even knew about it. He said "Well it might surprise you to know that so am I". He said, however, "I don't think either of us are going to get it, a greyhound man is going to get it so if you fancy being a promoter why don't you come in with me at Hackney". So I gave him £1,000 for a half share to run in 1964, which was the year of the black when we ran outside the Speedway Control Board. I was still riding and very much involved as a rider getting that season's Provincial League programme off the ground.'

Was he worried that the dispute would spiral out of control? 'No, I never did think much of the Speedway Control Board anyway and I've always been a bit of a rebel so it suited me. Because I was co-promoter, I felt it only right that I should ride for Hackney, so we arranged a transfer deal taking David Crane to Exeter and me to Hackney. So I became rider/promoter and I had not been there very long and I had a bad accident, and broke my wrist and shoulder. It was Dennis Day and Howdy Byford and me. I think I was between them and Dennis didn't turn. Took us all for a ride and I was catapulted over the fence.'

Len never rode competitively again. 'So since I couldn't ride I started concentrating on the management side. That season we lost £3,000 and Mike Parker wanted to shut it but I didn't. I felt that with the new British League being formed and having the top clubs there that I could make a go of it. Anyway, he wasn't having none of it and he was adamant that we were going to shut it and I was just as adamant that we weren't. I bought his share for £300 and became sole promoter and we went from there.'

It was being the sole man in charge that his flair for promoting came to fruition. Len would leave no stone unturned to promote the team. Leaflet campaigns were only the start; Len even purchased some old coaches to run buses on race nights to Waterden Road. It was tough going though, and on more than one occasion Len found himself in financial difficulty trying to keep the Hawks alive. In the end all the hard work paid off and Len went on to run Hackney successfully for twenty years.

However, success was few and far between – at least results-wise – but where Hackney fans were the richest of all was the racing that Len served up every week. The track surface and banking were always excellently prepared, making the track a visiting riders' paradise and perhaps accounting in part for the lack of team success. Silver recalls: 'It was legendary but it wasn't always like that. When I went there it was know as "Agony Wick" 'cos it was so bumpy and tough – it was awful. I knew nothing about tracks and had never done one in my life so my first job was to make it smooth. I discovered that the reason why it was bumpy was the base of the track was made of clinker and big lumps too. The clinker tended to move and break out, leaving a hole which very quickly became a big hole. So the first thing I do is to go round the riding line on the inside and get out all the old clinker out fairly quickly. It became fairly smooth although not nice to ride. At the end of that season I made me mind up to totally change the track. The amazing thing was that we did it all by hand.

Len Silver on the terraces serving his ban complete with the essential Hackney fan kit of programme board, hat and scarf.

I lowered the white line by about a foot. Jackie Biggs helped me do it. He was a bloody human dynamo, wonderful man Jack. All the material that came out we put on the outside and we immediately had two foot of banking. By the time we got some shale on it, it very quickly built up. The level of the track was a straight line: from white line to fence the angle was exactly the same, so wherever you rode you had the same angle and that's why the track was so good and you could ride it so many different ways and be successful. And that was made the Hackney track the best racetrack in the country, bar none.' Len's reputation for preparing excellent surfaces was acknowledged when he became tasked with preparing the Wembley track for the one-off World Championship events in the 1970s and '80s.

Controversy did follow him around though and by his own admission he was a rebel. What exactly did happen at Swindon in 1976 to earn him a ban? He laughs loudly: 'It was an incident involving Zenon Plech. Round the pits turn Zenon was neck and neck with their rider, although I can't remember who it was, and he ran the bloke wide. Zenon didn't put him in the fence; in fact the bloke never fell off. Perfectly legitimate. The referee disqualified Zenon for boring [the term used at the time for riding hard under someone]. I went berserk. I went up into the referee's box and I can still see him now. He was perched on a little stool looking all smug [he laughs again] so I thumped him and he went down like a pack of cards. I ended up banned, so for that period I got myself a yellow and blue scarf and walked round the dog-track cheering and everything. I loved it.'

Rather than pay ludicrous transfer fees, Len tried hard to produce home-grown talent and started the Hackney training school in 1971. 'Hackney would have had a fabulous team of kids that could have won the league several times over but they all got injured. Alan Emmett, Graham Miles and Dave Kennett all spring to mind, but bad crashes put paid to that.' What about Len's riders? He grins with obvious affection: 'Barry Thomas, lovely man. He drank too much then, he could have been so much better than he was. He came to me from Canterbury in a swap deal with Graeme Smith. I can't remember why we did the swap deal and Johnnie Hoskins, who was a good friend, and I agreed to bring Barry to Hackney.'

We look at the 1969 statistics and Len sees that Smith's average was 3.10. 'That's why I did it! Barry of course was an instant hit. I remember his very first meeting – it was astonishing. His bike looked as if it had square wheels 'cos he was wobbling all over the place and blasting round the fence and the public took to him instantly. A great character but he wasn't the only one – we had some lovely people at Hackney over the years. Zenon Plech, beautiful guy. Very few people know this but I first got Zenon Plech by smuggling him out of Europe and into England in the boot of my car. These were the days of Communism in Poland and thinking back I can't think what possessed me but we did it. It was from the World Team Cup in Norden in 1975 and he came home with me and going through the docks he got into the boot of the car as he had no legal way of getting into England. He came to live with me and I tried to adopt him legally so he became a British citizen. He wanted to do it because he

Silver interrupts Thommo's tea.

was just like a son to me but he wouldn't because he felt there would be repercussions on his family back in Poland if he did. So we never did it, but he was a great guy. One of the greatest ever riders was Bengt Jansson. Another lovely man, the nicest Swede of them all.

I was always lucky over the years with the riders that rode for me: they were all nice people. Good friends. I never had much aggravation, even with Garry Middleton. Now he came to me with a reputation as a real troublemaker which he had been, no doubt about that, but I have to say that he was larger than life, a superb character and good for the crowd – but he was no aggravation to me, apart from that every now and then he would use my office phone to call Australia or New Zealand! There were several incidents that could have blown up into trouble. There was the famous time up at Cradley Heath that he pulled a gun out of his toolbox and threatened Roy Trigg with it. Everyone thought it was hilarious.

Colin Pratt came to Hackney in 1964 and stayed with us and became one of our best scoring men. He never used to move off the white line, we had round Hackney what we used to call "Pratty's Groove" – he had a line and only he could get in it. He was a great trapper but was never guilty of passing anyone, but he scored lots of points and again he was very popular and beat lots of star men constantly. But he disappointed me at the end when he went to Cradley for money. They offered him some fantastic deal which I couldn't afford to pay and of course you can't blame him but I felt hurt at the time because he was the only rider who ever left me for another promoter over money. We of course got Bob Andrews, but he was never a Colin Pratt.

Finn Thomsen, yet another great guy. Brilliant mechanic, he had the quickest engines in the world. He was such a professional. With Finn everything had to be exact. Bo Petersen came over as a kid and he too became one of our top scorers, another lovely man. But I mustn't forget the old school, Les McGillivray, Jackie Biggs and Gerald Jackson. I knew them all for years. Les was a damn good rider, Gerald Jackson was a great engine tuner but for me the outstanding one was Jackie Biggs.'

So who was the best ever Hackney Rider? 'Two riders stand out in my mind: Bengt Jansson and Zenon Plech. Bengt Jansson was the classiest rider in the world. His throttle control was magnificent and he was famous for his last-bend swoops, up the banking and straight down across the line to beat people over the line. He did that time and time again. Zenon he was just an astonishing rider. In many ways he was like Gollob is today, squaring off the corner, going entirely in the wrong direction, pass someone and then carry on. They seemed like ridiculous things. He would ride underneath somebody without turning at all and you'd think "God, he's going into the fence" and then he would be round and away he went. As a racer there was no harder rider in the business. I mean Zenon never ever did anything other than flat out race for four laps. If you beat Zenon you had to work bloody hard for it. He was tenacious.

Those two in terms of ability were the best, and of course they both finished second in the World Championship and they both should have won. On each occasion they were robbed. Banger by SVEMO, who instructed him to let Fundin win it [1967 World Final] which I think was disgraceful but if he hadn't of done he would have been in trouble, but he was the winner on the night, no question about it, he was the outstanding rider. Then there was the night Zenon should have won it in Poland [1979 World Final]. Again he was the outstanding rider on the night. He was the only rider to have come from the back. He lined up against Mauger and Kelly Moran and the start was the biggest disgrace I have ever seen in a major event. As they came up to the tapes, Mauger was at the tapes first and Zenon was 10 yards behind. The tapes went up and Zenon was stranded. It was ridiculous. We all thought they would stop it but they didn't.'

And Len's greatest moment? Without hesitation, he answers: 'When Barry Thomas beat Ivan Mauger. Astonishing. There was also a number of races between Bengt Jansson and Sverre Harfeldt of West Ham. When Sverre used to ride round the fence and Bengt used to ride round the inside or the middle and they were absolutely tied together for four laps. Whenever West Ham came it was always a classic between two great riders.

'Another favourite moment was the 1978 Jubilee meeting. Personally I am very proud of the fact that I put more people into that stadium than it had ever seen in its whole history from the day it was built. We put 14,000 people in there and there were another 2,000 who couldn't get there because they were snowed in. I was also the last promoter ever to pay Jack Parker to ride a speedway bike – he was seventy-one. Loads of other promoters tried that year to get Jack to do it but he wouldn't.'

It is clear that Len saw Hackney as one big family and put a lot into his relationship with the riders. That must have made it doubly difficult when Vic Harding was lost? Len's eyes water and his voice cracks – 'Terrible'. It is obvious that he is still deeply affected by what happened. 'Awful. What was so upsetting was that we had already put up a very high safety fence to avoid exactly that kind of accident. They cleared it and went way over the top of it. I have never seen a rider go so high. It was just incredible. He was ten foot up in the air. And they went by the lamp-post and I can see it in my mind's eye, his head hit it, the lamp-post, and I knew he was dead instantly. Nobody could have survived that.'

At the end of the 1983 season the news that Len was quitting his beloved Hackney shocked all at the Wick. 'I quit for a group of reasons, not one solitary reason. It was losing money, but then it had lost and earned money over the years. My landlord then was George Walker. I had spoken to him at the end of 1982 and told him that this place is losing money and I cannot continue in the existing way, we have to do something about the rent – because I used to pay them lots of money for rent, lots of money. I really need you to review that and if you want me to stay there then you are going to have to review the rent.

'He was all very kind, "Don't worry, we'll do that" and the winter came and I set my stall out for the next season on that basis. I kept trying to see him and he was giving me the run around; he kept on cancelling appointments I had with him until finally until a week before the season opened and I finally got to see him and instead of putting the rent down he put it up. So I said "Do be aware that I can't afford that and I will not be there forever," and that was a major factor in making me decide to move on. Funnily enough, the people that followed me in got a much better rental deal, probably because when he lost me he realised I meant it. Also I got divorced and started my skiing company at that time, so it came together. It was a sad day for me because it had been my life for twenty-odd years and it was sad way to end it.

'Chris Shears signed a contract with me to buy the assets of Hackney Speedway. He revoked on that contract and brought a share in Ipswich. I threatened to sue and he settled out of court for a substantial sum of money, because had it gone to court he would have lost a lot of money. I then sold the licence and some of the riders to Oxford and the rest of the bits and bobs I sold to Terry Russell, who brought the Kestrels over. It cost him a lot of money not to do it.'

But can speedway ever return to the Wick? 'I think it's unlikely but not impossible. At the moment the stadium is standing derelict and it would take a very brave man to open the stadium for anything, because the amount of money it would require to resurrect it to a usable state would be phenomenal.'

Looking back from today's perspective, Len Silver was the last of the great promoters – arguably the greatest since Johnnie Hoskins. From booking stunt rider Eddie Kidd to jump the Hawks to giving away free rock to the kids at the end of the season, Len had an unforgettable style. How many of today's fans patiently waited for a chance to grab the lucky fifty-pence piece, which was used to toss for gate positions by the two team captains, before being thrown into the assembled crowd of children. On one occasion the car from the film *Death Race 2002* was displayed and also, at a time when speedway rarely got onto the television, Len succeeded in persuading Thames Television to transmit a live five-heat individual event prior to the main meeting during their thirty-minute Friday night sports programme. Fortunately, he returned to speedway and is back running his 'other' team, Rye House.

1984 – Return Of The Maestro

During the winter Chris Shears had a dramatic change of mind, putting Hackney's very future at risk. Fortunately, for Hackney at least, across the Thames at Crayford in Kent, Ladbrokes had decided to redevelop the greyhound stadium that housed the Crayford Kestrels. The promoter, Terry Russell, who was concerned that he had no guarantee about the future at London Road, immediately decided to transfer the whole operation to Waterden Road. A condition of getting a new licence was that the lamp standards that had caused the deaths of Harding and Pyeatt were moved back from the perimeter of the safety fence, but the banking stayed – albeit slightly reduced – and, despite the loss of so-called superstars visiting the circuit, the scene was set for more of the same excellent racing always enjoyed at the Wick but on a slightly altered 320-yard circuit.

Of course for many Hawks fans the loss of British League racing was a bitter pill to swallow. To add insult to injury, an attempt was to integrate the two clubs and the team name was changed from the Hawks to the Kestrels. Many fans left, never to return. But it was their loss and, with a large Crayford contingent making the transition successfully, the future looked rosy. The Crayford team was very young and had reached the 1983 Super National Final before losing to Newcastle. With Malcolm Simmons as the team manager there was optimism that the youngsters' potential would be realised.

They did have one very experienced rider and he was a Hackney legend – his name was Barry Thomas. For those old Hawks fans determined to stick with the team, the return of the ever-popular Thomas went a long way to ensuring their continued support. Of course Thomas had never truly left, having had three successful years as number eight to supplement the eleven full-time seasons preceding that. Backing him were several youngsters with enormous potential, many of whom were protégés of Thomas and had learned their trade at his Iwade training track.

Andy Galvin at eighteen had impressed in his first seasons at Crayford, as had twenty-two-year-old Paul Bosley. Kevin Teager (25) and grass-track star Trevor Banks (28) were also retained from the previous year. Unfortunately, the Kestrels had fallen foul of the points limit and there was no place for Alan Mogridge or Alan Sage from the previous season's line-up. The points limit had been introduced several season earlier to control team strengths and to ensure a more evenly balanced league. It had never been of concern to Hackney before, but now it was to play an important part in the future. Sage was loaned to newly-formed Arena Essex and Mogridge was to go on loan to a variety of clubs during the season.

Replacing those two were two newcomers. Mark Terry and the highly rated Paul Whittaker, who actually celebrated his sixteenth birthday on Hackney's opening night, 23 March, in a challenge match against Mildenhall. Although most of the team were new and unfamiliar, it was like old times as Barry Thomas, lining up for his fifteenth season for Hackney and back as skipper, started the first heat. He did not disappoint and roared home to open the new era at the Wick.

The riders had no home advantage, seeing as this was their first performance at the circuit, but an excellent match ensued. The Kestrels opened up an 8-point lead, but Mildenhall gradually clawed it back and, with one heat to go, Hackney were leading 37-35. Paul Bosley was having an excellent debut and had scored 8 points from his first three rides, but as the green light came on for the decider he nudged the tapes and was excluded. Enter Paul Whittaker. He had won his first ride and had done well on his opening performance, but to find himself in a final-heat decider on his debut must have been daunting. His partner was Andy Galvin, who had not had a happy opening meeting, but the two youngsters (not for the last time in Hackney colours) managed second and third places for a very enjoyable opening win 40-38.

Fortunately the riders weighed the track up very quickly. Rye House, still controlled by Len Silver, were dispatched in the first round of the cup, Hackney winning both home and away, with Paul Bosley becoming the first to score a maximum and Hackney scored an early away league win too, after a Thomas' last-heat victory secured a 40-38 result at Weymouth. After winning their opening nine matches, Hackney were defeated for the first time away to Mildenhall in the cup 34-44, although the result was amended to 33-45 after Kevin Teager took an illegal ride in heat 8. The first major test came on

18 May. Could the new-look Kestrels come back from a 12-point deficient to progress any further in the cup? The answer was a resounded yes as Hackney won on the night 51-27, moving through to the semi-final. Hackney were easily beaten at both Edinburgh and Berwick and this was to start a complete loss of away form – which was not helped when they lost Paul Bosley with broken bones in his hand when defeating Rye House at home on 1 June. Thomas won the Hartsman Lager Chase (formerly Hackney's Champions Chase) meeting on 3 June at Rye House and celebrated with a maximum three days later during the 47-31 home victory over Edinburgh.

Hackney qualified for the National League Four-Team Tournament final, finishing as winners on aggregate by beating Canterbury, Weymouth and Arena Essex. Mark Terry was replaced by Linden Warner, who made his debut in a controversial away defeat at Peterborough, where the home riders did most of their overtaking by crossing the non-existent white line. Having failed to win an away match since the opening one at Weymouth nine away fixtures ago, a home defeat on 6 July against Mildenhall effectively ended Hackney's league aspirations. It seemed that the consistency problem that beset the Hawks was now affecting the Kestrels. Both Thomas and Banks were struggling with the new clampdown on riders moving at the starting gate and were losing points. Critically, both had earned exclusions in heats 11 and 12 against Mildenhall. This

Hackney, 1984 Knockout Cup Champions. From left to right, back row: Dave Pavitt, Trevor Banks, Kevin Teager, Linden Warner, Paul Bosley, Terry Russell. Front row: Andy Galvin, Barry Thomas, Paul Whittaker.

The winning skipper receives the Knockout Cup Trophy.

clampdown was a constant source of annoyance for the fans as referees were not consistent in their application of the new rule. Some excluded if you barely moved but others would allow rolling at the start as long as the tapes were not pushed.

Hackney staged the National League Pairs competition and, represented by Thomas and Banks, failed to reach the latter stages, despite two maximum heat scores in the qualifiers. Stoke were the eventual winners.

The final of the Four-Team Tournament was staged at Peterborough on 22 July, but Hackney finished last in their semi-final, leaving the Kestrels with only the cup as potential silverware.

Hackney lined up for the most important match of the season, the cup semi-final against Peterborough, on 27 August. Hackney were rampant with Thomas, Bosley and Teager unbeaten, they chalked up a 30-point lead to take to the second leg held on 7 September. Peterborough were determined to pull off the comeback of the season. The Hackney riders struggled and, when they did hit the front, the Peterborough riders simply rode round the inside on the grass and overtook. Five 5-1s and two 4-2s saw Peterborough leading 9-33 with the aggregate lead reduced to 6 points. Two successive wins for Trevor Banks stemmed the tide a little, but another 1-5 in heat 10 (after Bosley's chain had snapped whilst leading) brought the Panthers only 4 points behind. Peterborough then objected that Thomas had an illegal tyre, despite the fact that he had finished last in heat 9.

Thomas was normally such a mild-mannered character, but had shown over the years to be more than capable of upping the stakes if wound up, and Peterborough may have unwittingly helped out in that with the tyre protest. Hackney held on grimly with Thomas and Teager providing the minor places in heat 11 and Bosley winning heat 12. So the scene was set for the last-heat aggregate decider. Thomas and Bosley were up against Mick Hines and Ian Barney; Peterborough needed a 5-1 to force a replay, Hackney needed to split them to sneak through. For the Hackney faithful, the tension was almost unbearable.

Mick Hines rocketed from the tapes and into the distance and Paul Bosley's engine blew, leaving Thomas and Peterborough track specialist Ian Barney to battle it out. Thomas was clearly fired up and riding as though his life depended on. He gave it everything he had and held on in second place. Having endured machinery trouble all night, the fans were wondering if the bike would hold out. In the end, after a truly dramatic meeting, Thomas crossed the line in second place and the success-starved Hackney fans could contain their emotion no longer. The crowd spilled onto the track as Thomas rode around to take his applause, and was lifted high into the sky being given the traditional bumps, whilst one fan sunk to his knees and kissed the bike. Hackney were through to the cup final by the slimmest of margins, losing on the night 25-53 but winning on aggregate 79-77.

The fans did not have long to wait for the final as, just two weeks later, Berwick were back in town to decide the destiny of the cup. Hackney again put in an impressive home performance and, with both Thomas and Banks scoring 11 points, emerged comfortable winners 46-32. The return leg was staged on 29 September and Kestrels were determined not to let a repeat of the Peterborough match spoil their last chance of success. However, from the start Hackney trailed and two 1-5s in heats 3 and 4 reduced the lead to only 6 points. But the Kestrels hit back and, fittingly, it was Thomas who clinched the cup for Hackney with second place in heat 10. He had been inspirational on the night, scoring 11 points, and had been in the Hackney team the last time they had won any major competition – the British League Knockout Cup in 1971. Hackney lost on the night 37-40, enough to secure the aggregate victory 83-72.

Trevor Banks had ridden well and definitely both his and Thomas' scoring would have been significantly higher if they had adapted better to the new tape laws. Kevin Teager also had a good season after taking a couple of meetings to get Hackney weighed up. Paul Bosley and Andy Galvin perhaps did not make the progress expected, but they were young and had time on their side. Paul Whittaker at sixteen did everything that could be expected. Linden Warner scored slightly better than the rider he replaced, Mark Terry, and certainly added a bit more strength to the reserve berth – particularly in the important heat 2. Thomas had revelled in his return and was like the Thommo of old as several thrilling from-the-back victories wound the clock back to the golden days of Hackney and, as if proof were needed, the cup campaign demonstrated what a great skipper he really was. He also represented Hackney in the NLRC, scoring 4 points.

Cup winners and fourth position in the league ensured that the lower sphere of racing had successfully been introduced to Waterden Road, along with the successful integration of two sets of fans. The points limit would dictate what happened next.

1984 National League Record (4/16 teams)

Played	Won	Drawn	Lost	For	Against	Pts
30	16	0	14	1,206	1,124	32

1984 Cup Record

Round 1	Rye House	Won 95-61
Round 2	Mildenhall	Won 84-72
Semi-final	Peterborough	Won 79-77
Final	Berwick	Won 83-72

1984 National League and Cup Averages (captain in italics)

Rider	Mts	Rds	Pts	BP	Total	CMA	Maxs
Trevor Banks	37	156	314	16	330	8.46	3
Barry Thomas	*38*	*165*	*328*	*20*	*348*	*8.44*	*3*
Kevin Teager	38	152	239	40	279	7.34	4
Paul Bosley	34	137	217	19	236	6.89	4
Andy Galvin	35	139	184	25	209	6.01	
Mark Terry	16	46	47	13	60	5.22	
Linden Warner	26	83	90	17	107	5.16	
Paul Whittaker	38	122	126	26	152	4.98	

1985 – What's The Points?

With all the permutations calculated to fit the points limit, Kevin Teager drew the short straw and was transferred to Wimbledon, with Alan Mogridge earning his recall. Linden Warner was recalled by his parent club Birmingham and was replaced by Richard Pettman from the Hackney junior squad. Those two changes added to the retained riders – Thomas, Banks, Bosley, Galvin and Whittaker – left Hackney with the majority of the cup-winning squad from the previous year trying to move four places up the league.

The season opened at Milton Keynes on 19 March and the Kestrels romped home to a 49-29 victory in a challenge match. Hopes were certainly high after a superlative performance, but the joy was short-lived as Wimbledon, who had just joined the National League, managed to win the London Cup by a single point.

The league campaign commenced at home to Middlesbrough on 12 April. The meeting was wet from outset and Middlesbrough, taking advantage of difficult track conditions that clearly did not suit the home riders, streaked into a 10-point lead after 6 heats. Alan Mogridge had clashed with Martin Dixon in a couple of races and some dubious refereeing decisions had not helped the Kestrels' cause. All seemed lost, but an electrical fault developed at the base of one of the lamp standards and, with the rain falling and the chance that the whole of the track lights might go off at any moment, the referee had no alternative but to abandon the meeting. Tempers were frayed and at one point, unusually for speedway fans, things looked set to boil over. The well-fancied 'Boro' Tigers team clearly felt that an excellent opportunity had been lost which may not re-present itself in the re-run.

The Kestrels won at Scunthorpe 41-36, beat Mildenhall in the cup for the second consecutive season and thrashed former sister track Rye House, 54-24. However, Scunthorpe dropped out of the league and with them went Hackney's two away league points, although Middlesbrough lost their appeal against the abandonment decision. To cut costs, the National League away matches were often paired such that teams rode on two or three successive nights. The first northern tour produced narrow defeats at Ellesmere Port and Berwick, split by a 45-33 victory at Edinburgh. Shortly after, a second trip up North saw cup success at Long Eaton, but Middlesbrough took full revenge for the earlier abandoned league match and won 28-50 – despite their main stand having burnt down the night before. Glasgow completed the tour, but Hackney lost again. Finally, the southern tour of Exeter and Poole resulted in two defeats.

One win from these 7 away matches and it looked like Hackney would again be prevented from mounting a serious league challenge due to poor away form. On 12 July, despite beating Long Eaton in the first part of a double header, Poole inflicted Hackney's first home defeat of the season; this killed any lingering hopes of league success.

The fours final was held at Peterborough on 21 July and the Kestrels won their semi-final beating illustrious opposition in Wimbledon, Berwick and Stoke before finishing a worthy third in the final – a real bonus considering the Kestrels' previous performances at the East of England Show Ground. The final had formed a marathon weekend of speedway as the day before the Grand Slam had been held also at Peterborough. Sixty heats of speedway (three traditional twenty-heat individual meetings consisting of two semi-finals and a final) were held. The qualifiers had been determined by scoring qualifying points in second half scratch races. Andy Galvin and Paul Bosley represented Hackney, Galvin riding magnificently to finish in a very credible second place.

The rerun with Middlesbrough resulted in an anticlimax and the Tigers were soundly beaten 48-29. The big concern was the form of skipper Thomas. His CMA was down to 7 points per match and he found himself at reserve after a run of mechanical problems had hit hard. Hackney again staged the National League Best Pairs on 15 September but again the home side, represented by Banks and Galvin, failed to make use of the advantage and failed to reach the semi-finals. Ellesmere Port went on to win the final and they would also provide the Kestrels' cup semi-final opponents

Just four days prior to the semi-final clash, Hackney were in action at Birmingham. Thomas, upset by poor performances, failed to turn up as Hackney won in his absence, 38-36. Retirement was actually discussed but Thomas was talked out of such a hasty decision and agreed to take his place in the cup semi-final that was held on successive nights over 26 and 27 September. Hackney had only narrowly lost at Ellesmere earlier in the season, but this time were overwhelmed 28-50 – leaving the team with a mountain to climb.

The Kestrels' hopes of victory received an unfortunate boost when the Gunners' Joe Owen was injured in heat 4 and took no further part in the meeting. The Kestrels set about pulling back the points. Heat 8 was a turning point when Galvin, trying too hard, fell whilst comfortably in third. But Hackney continued to pull back the deficit, led by a rejuvenated Thomas who had put his problems behind him, and with one race to go Hackney required a 5-1 in the last heat to force a replay. The crowd, sensing a chance, starting chanting 'Thommo, Thommo'. He had scored 11 from the reserve berth and was eligible for another race. He was duly brought in to partner Whittaker, against his old team-mate Dave Morton and Dave Walsh. Whittaker sped from the tapes to secure victory, but Walsh managed to get into second place. Thomas tried everything for the first two laps, but then his engine started to misfire and it was all he could do to keep Morton behind him. Hackney's hero from the previous season's semi-final could not repeat the performance, but the ever-popular Thomas was still given a hero's welcome for his efforts. In the end, the failure was almost certainly down to a first heat 1-5, ex-Hawk Dave Morton scoring a valuable win. Hackney had won on the night 49-29 but had gone out of the cup 77-79 on aggregate.

A season that had promised so much finished without any silverware. Hackney's away form had let them down but they could take comfort from the fact that many of their riders were still very young and still had a way to go to achieve their full potential. Banks again finished as top scorer – a reliable performer who frustratingly had 'off races' he finished a creditable third in the NLRC. Andy Galvin had considerably improved and at last looked as though he was progressing towards his obvious potential. Engine problems were his biggest downfall. Paul Whittaker, who had improved to become the third heat leader, also looked like becoming a star name. Mogridge, like Banks, had good and bad meetings but had effectively matched Teager's scoring. Paul Bosley was without doubt very talented, but he was also a complete enigma, scoring a maximum one week and 2 points the next. Thomas' scoring was down, but he was always an inspirational captain, which is so important to such a young side. Richard Pettman had not pulled up any trees but had had a satisfactory first year and had done as much as could have been expected.

Again the line-up for the following year would depend on the viable permutations of the averages, but it would surely not be long before Hackney's young team delivered the goods.

The enigmatic Paul Bosley.

1985 National League Record (5/16 teams)

Played	Won	Drawn	Lost	For	Against	Pts
36	22	0	14	1,544	1,251	44

1985 Cup Record

Round 1	Bye	
Round 2	Mildenhall	Won 79-76
Round 3	Long Eaton	Won 92-64
Semi-final	Ellesmere Port	Lost 77-79

1985 National League and Cup Averages (captain in italics)

Rider	Mts	Rds	Pts	BP	Total	CMA	Maxs
Trevor Banks	41	171	314	36	350	8.19	5
Andy Galvin	42	173	307	40	347	8.02	8
Paul Whittaker	42	150	266	25	291	7.76	3
Paul Bosley	39	151	250	34	284	7.52	6
Alan Mogridge	42	165	257	45	302	7.32	3
Barry Thomas	*40*	*164*	*274*	*25*	*299*	*7.29*	*2*
Richard Pettman	42	114	115	27	142	4.98	

1986 – Homing Hawk

With Hackney finishing the previous season with a cumulative points total of 52, it was obvious that yet again changes would be forced upon the Kestrels, with at least two having to be released. Terry Russell and his fellow promoter Dave Pavitt had decided that the lack of a high-scoring number one was the least of Hackney's problems. The rider they signed was ex-Hawk Malcolm Simmons, returning to the Hackney line-up for the first time since 1963. Making way was Trevor Banks, who must have wondered what he had done wrong to top the scorechart for two successive seasons and still be transferred. Banks joined Milton Keynes and, in another shock move, Paul Bosley announced his sudden and premature retirement. Alan Mogridge was also a victim of the cull, transferring to Canterbury to accommodate Simmons 11-point assessed CMA.

Much was expected of Galvin and Whittaker and, if Thomas could score at more or less the same rate, then the strong Hackney top four could perhaps be strong enough to carry the rest – reserves Pettman, Gary Rolls and Carl Chalcraft. From the outset, it looked dangerously like the gamble would backfire. Simmons immediately started scoring as per his average, flying to a 15-point maximum in the first leg of the London Cup at Wimbledon. But with only Thomas in support, Hackney went down 35-42 and then lost at home on 28 March to a Rye House team now run by Russell's brother, Ronnie.

A single point won the London Cup seven days later, Wimbledon being beaten 43-35 and in a turnaround of fortunes Hackney won the return match at Rye House 49-29, ensuring aggregate success by 86-70. Former Rye rider Gary Rolls, scored a valuable 10

points, whilst both Simmons and Thomas raced to maximums – a feat they repeated the following week against Exeter at Waterden Road, proving that Hackney was top heavy. The cup again offered the biggest hope of glory for the Kestrels and Rye House were beaten 83-72 on aggregate, despite missing Simmons from the away leg after he was called up to appear in the Overseas Final.

Hackney collected their first away league points of the year on 9 July at Long Eaton. The victory was all the more remarkable since Hackney lost the services of Simmons in heat 5 with a broken collarbone, having crashed with the Invaders John Proctor. The injury

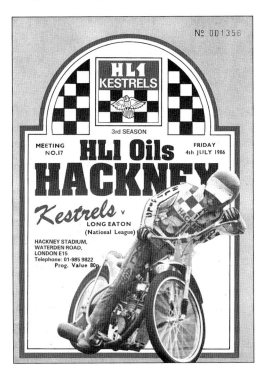

1986 programme.

National League Pairs runners-up.

would dent Hackney's chances of winning the National League Pairs Championship, again held at Waterden Road, four days later. Thomas replaced Simmons and, paired with Galvin, rose to the occasion magnificently. The tournament used a unique scoring system of 4-3-2-0 to encourage team riding, giving a pairing in 2nd/3rd place a higher score than a pair in 1st/4th. Hackney qualified for the semi-finals after scoring 7-2s over Exeter and Boston and a 6-3 over Berwick. In the semis they met Mildenhall who, like Hackney, had signed their own 'big gun' from the British League. Dave Jessup predictably led from start to finish but, with Thomas and Galvin in the minor places after Jessup's partner Eric Monaghan fell and was excluded, Hackney moved into the final where they met Edinburgh.

Les Collins had been riding well, but the Hackney pairing could be expected to beat his partner Doug Wyer. Collins led from the start with Thomas second and Wyer third. However, Galvin fell trying to pass and was excluded, leaving Thomas on his own with no mathematical chance in the re-run. Hackney's last remaining hopes for honours evaporated when neighbours Arena Essex dumped the Kestrels out of the cup. Simmons was missing from the first leg at Purfleet on 17 July, but the remaining riders restricted the Hammers to an 8-point lead. Even with Simmons' return for the second leg on 1 August, the Kestrels could only manage a draw through a final-heat 5-1 from Thomas and Galvin.

The final hope of success rested on the fours finals on 10 August. The Kestrels came second in their semi-final to Poole, despite losing Thomas after a nasty spill involving Stoke's Tom Owen in heat 3. Owen was leading with Thomas a close second and seemingly likely to overtake, but Owen fell on turn four leaving Thomas nowhere to go – both men and their machines went flying. Thomas sustained concussion and did not take any further part in the meeting. The Kestrels finished third in the final, rueing what may have been had Thomas not been lost. 'I tried to go over the fence there once! I always had a bit of rivalry going with him [Owen] 'cos we were a couple of old codgers!'

Alan Mogridge made a late-season return (since the Kestrels' averages were now low enough to accommodate him) but that did little to help. A third of the home matches were lost and Hackney slumped to thirteenth place, despite a late victory at Boston on 25 October. Simmons had done well and finished fourth in the NLRC. However, the gamble of his inclusion never paid off and, with Galvin not improving as much as required and Whittaker having a poor season, the Kestrels had their worst campaign for a long time. Thomas had improved with the added responsibility of riding in a struggling team, but the remainder of the team predictably floundered.

Rumours had been circulating for a while that Russell and Pavitt had been contemplating a move back into the British League. Opinion was divided as to whether this was a good idea or not, especially given the climate of the time. One thing was for certain, whatever league Hackney competed in, the team would include their mascot for 1986, a young man called Mark Loram.

Malcolm Simmons with the Silver Helmet.

1986 National League Record (13/20 teams)

Played	Won	Drawn	Lost	For	Against	Pts
38	16	0	22	1,433	1,517	32

1986 Cup Record

Round 1	Bye	
Round 2	Rye House	Won 83-72
Round 3	Arena Essex	Lost 74-82

1986 National League and Cup Averages (captain in italics)

Rider	Mts	Rds	Pts	BP	Total	CMA	Maxs
Malcolm Simmons	38	165	391	9	400	9.70	10
Andy Galvin	40	168	318	16	334	7.95	2
Barry Thomas	*42*	*183*	*314*	*24*	*338*	*7.39*	*3*
Alan Mogridge	7	30	42	8	50	6.67	
Paul Whittaker	42	172	223	47	270	6.28	1
Gary Rolls	33	115	91	26	117	4.07	
Carl Chalcraft	33	91	72	17	89	3.91	
Richard Pettman	39	128	109	12	121	3.78	
Mike Fitspatrick	7	21	17	2	19	3.62	
Steve Smith	8	18	6	1	7	1.56	

1987 – Back With The Big Boys

Hackney did return to the British League and it was change all the way. Obviously a major signing was going to be necessary and that was England captain Simon Wigg, who wanted to establish himself as an outright number one, having been in Hans Nielsen's shadow at Oxford. Malcolm Simmons was retained as the new skipper and returned to the senior league in his twenty-fifth season in speedway. At the other end of the scale was Mark Loram, joining the team at sixteen years of age and getting a baptism of fire. The Kestrels also looked abroad for talent and signed a little-known Dane, Allan Johanssen, and rookie American Randy Green. Completing the team was Andy Galvin and, surprisingly, Alan Mogridge, whilst Barry Thomas was back again as number eight whilst continuing his National League career with Rye House.

There were changes on the management side too. Terry Russell had bowed out, leaving Dave Pavitt alone at the helm, but another England international, John Louis, was recruited to takeover Simmons' team-manager role. Challenge matches opened Hackney's return and, though they struggled away, the team at least won at home, giving some optimism that they could have a reasonable season.

Allan Johansson.

The league cup campaign opened with two away defeats at Reading and Sheffield and Coventry managed to snatch a draw at Waterden Road. Good Friday brought a return to the traditional home-and-away clashes with Ipswich. The away fixture at Foxhall Heath in the afternoon proved satisfactory in that the Kestrels went down by only 8 points. However, Alan Mogridge damaged ligaments in his foot and would miss that evening's return. Barry Thomas was called up to replace him and in true fashion scored a spectacular 8 points, which sadly did not stop the Witches completing the double 37-41. The following night Hackney were crushed at Cradley and that prompted Pavitt to immediately strengthen the side. Again he looked abroad and signed young Swedish star Roland Danno. Danno made his debut on 24 April, but the Kestrels lost again at home to Sheffield 35-43.

Despite an away win at Bradford, there was disquiet on the terraces: many had not been keen to return to the British League and certainly not to struggle. Wigg was scoring well but Simmons was struggling, especially away from home. Apart from Galvin, who had achieved an impressive CMA of 7 points per match, the others were taking their time to feel their way – although to be fair, Loram, Johnassen and Danno were riding well for their first season at this level. Green seemed way off the pace though and a fit-again Mogridge replaced him.

Hackney, 1987. From left to right, back row: Alan Mogridge, Barry Thomas, Dave Pavitt, Allan Johansson, Andy Galvin, Mike Western, John Louis. Front row: Mark Loram, Roland Danno. Simon Wigg is seated on the bike.

Roland Danno, who was sadly later confined to a wheelchair following an on-track accident.

Hackney won their first league match at home to Swindon 40-38, but lost Simmons with a dislocated shoulder less than a fortnight before his Silver Jubilee meeting. That meeting took place on 9 August and 'The Scandinavians' beat 'Malcolm's Bulldogs' and a 'World Select'. Simmons bravely tried to ride but, in obvious discomfort, he pulled out after his first outing and did not ride again that season. Barry Thomas was brought in to replace Simmons and, especially at home, immediately started to score well. Cradley were beaten 41-36 with Thommo scoring 8. The highlight of the meeting was a 5-1 from a team-riding Galvin and Mogridge over former World Champion Erik Gundersen in heat 5. In the next three home matches, Thomas continued to impress scoring 9 paid 11, 5, and 8.

When Ipswich arrived on 11 September, the feelings of the fans started to boil over again. Everyone knew Thomas was best from the outside gate. The banking allowed him to compensate for his notorious slow starting by sweeping around the outside on the first bend. At number two, Thomas found himself partnering Wigg in three of his four rides. He won heat 1 from the outside and Wigg could only manage third. Next time out, Wigg chose three and Thomas, stuck on the inside, could only manage third. Thomas won his next outing again from the outside in heat 8, but in his final outing, at a crucial stage in the match, he was last, having again had to start from the inside to allow Wigg to take the outside. Hackney only managed a draw against the old enemy and a section of the fans were blaming Wigg for not playing the captain's part in gate selection. After the match, team manager Louis was challenged by a group of fans asking why, when it was so obvious that Thomas scored more when starting from the outside, did Louis not insist that Wigg start from the inside. Louis, to his credit, offered no excuses stating that there was nothing that he could do as Wigg was the star rider and he therefore had the call on the gate positions. Wigg had not really settled at Waterden Road or sustained his early form. He was still scoring well, but the odd surprise defeat crept in along the way – sometimes making the difference between victory and defeat.

The season drew to an end with a whimper rather than a bang and few were sad it was over. There was very little to show by way of successes – in fact the only silverware was the one-legged London Cup victory at Wimbledon. The star of the show was Roland Danno. His scoring was little short of phenomenal and he quickly found himself promoted to the number one position. Mark Loram looked a real star for the future and had certainly had a successful first season. Andy Galvin had improved again and had done well on stepping up a league, whilst Allan Johanssen had tried hard. Mogridge, Simmons and Green were disappointing and Wigg never really achieved his objectives, having at last been given centre stage. He scored 7 points in the BLRC.

With twelve teams in the British League, Hackney finished tenth in the League Cup and ninth in the league. Pavitt's gamble had not paid off. He had not been helped by the fact that, in the National League, Hackney was surrounded by local teams Arena Essex, Rye House and Wimbledon. During the season a consortium had been assembled to help run Hackney, and Pavitt had been joined by Mike Western and Garry Muckley. As the close season commenced rumours were rife that the new consortium were taking Hackney straight back to the National League.

1987 British League Record (13/20 teams)

Played	Won	Drawn	Lost	For	Against	Pts
38	16	0	22	1,433	1,517	32

1987 Cup Record

Round 1	Bradford	Lost 89-91

1987 British League, League Cup and Cup Averages (captain in italics)

Rider	Mts	Rds	Pts	BP	Total	CMA	Maxs
Simon Wigg	45	211	476	19	495	9.38	6
Roland Danno	35	148	239	21	260	7.03	
Andy Galvin	42	177	231	39	270	6.10	
Allan Johansen	42	165	207	24	231	5.60	
Malcolm Simmons	*25*	*97*	*121*	*10*	*131*	*5.40*	
Alan Mogridge	42	154	168	33	201	5.22	
Barry Thomas	15	50	54	11	65	5.20	
Mark Loram	45	129	133	31	164	5.09	
Randy Green	6	19	10	2	12	2.53	

1988 – Year of the Kestrel

Hackney returned to the National League after the British League Management committee, despite assurances to the contrary, failed to impose a points limit on heat leaders. With Wigg rejoining Oxford, that only left Roland Danno as an established heat leader and, with no incentive for clubs to release heat leaders, the Hackney consortium felt that another uncompetitive season would be disastrous. The decision was announced to the fans at a public meeting on 14 December 1987. Any fears of upset were quelled as the huge gathering quickly rallied behind the promotion.

Hackney was able to reassemble a useful-looking team, almost exclusively from their own resources. Galvin was back and given the captaincy, as it was felt that the extra responsibility would do him good. Mogridge and Loram also dropped down and remained with the team. Much was expected of these three having had a season of British League experience. Paul Whittaker was recalled from Canterbury and, still only twenty years old, he had time for further improvements, while Barry Thomas was also recalled full time, for his nineteenth season in Hackney colours after a successful year on loan at Rye House (where he was voted Rider of the Year). With that strong top five, Hackney signed eighteen-year-old Chris Louis, son of team manager and former world number three, John. The final place went to Gary Rolls.

The full story about Thomas' inclusion has never been revealed. It represented the author's own personal moment of fame and therefore is indulged here. I attended the first of two pre-season practice sessions and was horrified that Thomas was not there. I, like many others, had assumed his recall from Rye House would be guaranteed. I was a friend of Dave Pickles who, a year earlier, had saved Wimbledon from closing down by organising a consortium of fans and he knew Pavitt. I asked him to enquire where Thomas was. Pavitt told him that he could not contact Thomas and that he had heard rumours that a sponsor was needed to make it financially viable for him to continue. Immediately, I asked what amount of money was required and set about raising as much of it as I could. A few days later, Pickles rang me to tell me that Pavitt had been in touch and that Thomas would ride if a sponsor could be found to prepare his bikes on a weekly basis. The pressure of Thomas' business was making it too difficult to continue with bike preparations. I was determined that Thommo should complete his twenty years of service at Hackney and so a message was sent back to Pavitt that the money was available and a week later Thomas was at the second pre-season practice and the deal had been done. In the end, I financed most of the money myself and – even though I felt my efforts went mostly unnoticed by the promotion – by the end of the season I was glad that I had.

Having beaten Glasgow and Eastbourne at Waterden Road, the Kestrels shocked everyone by winning at Exeter on 25 April. It was always difficult to win at Exeter's huge track and Hackney were delighted to win 49-47, coming from 12 points behind and scoring two 5-1s in the last two heats to win. Galvin looked like a different rider and Loram was also in a class of his own. Unlike other years, however, the remainder of the team was scoring well too. Louis was the star of an away win at Glasgow, scoring 14 in the 50-46 triumph which was only his fourth official match.

Chris Louis.

Andy Galvin and Mark Loram in love!

Hackney beat Poole in the cup, despite suffering their first defeat of the season at Wimborne Road 40-56, and a win at Eastbourne followed, with the Kestrels' strength in depth showing when Thomas took his turn to star, scoring 10. With home wins against Stoke and Long Eaton, Hackney were unbeaten in their first 8 league matches. Early June saw the Kestrels easily make it through the final of the Four-Team Championship, beating local rivals Mildenhall, Arena Essex and Rye House. Chris Louis' form was sensational and he moved into the team proper at the expense of Whittaker, who dropped to reserve.

Hackney marched on with wins at home against Exeter and Poole, a massive 61-33 win at Rye House – where only former Hawk Jens Rasmussen offered any resistance – and home-and-away wins over Milton Keynes. Hackney's first visit of the season to London rivals Wimbledon followed on 13 July. Hackney's nemesis John Berry was now team manager at Wimbledon and the rivalry was as strong as ever. Hackney dropped their first league point of the season when Galvin suffered engine failure on the last bend of the last heat (when in a match-winning second place), giving the Dons a gift draw.

A home victory two nights later over Rye House saw the Kestrels reach the halfway point in their league campaign still unbeaten after 15 matches and leading the table from Berwick by 5 points and Wimbledon by 8. Further home wins against Mildenhall and Arena Essex followed, but Poole repeated their cup success and inflicted Hackney's first away league defeat of the season on 19 July, 47-49.

Hackney duly dispatched Middlesbrough and moved into the semi-finals of the cup by winning the return cup clash 51-45 on 4 August and, the following night, they took on Peterborough in the league. Hackney were comfortably ahead 22-14 after six heats. In heat 7, Mark Loram and Peterborough's Mick Poole collided and fell. Poole was excluded and Loram won the re-run, but Mark's wrist was hurting and the track doctor diagnosed a broken scaphoid. Would the old Hackney injury jinx prove so costly again? Vital matches were scheduled in August, including the cup semi-final. The rest of the team now had to show their worth.

On 7 August the four-team final was held at Peterborough, but without Loram and no guests or rider replacement allowed, Hackney not surprisingly ducked out at their first semi-final. More importantly they had the away match at Mildenhall three days later. It was going to be tough in any event but without Loram it looked extremely daunting indeed. Rider replacement was operated in his absence and Hackney moved into a 6-point lead. However, two 5-1s brought the home side to within 2 points of Hackney before the match-winning performance came from Thomas. First he teamed up with Galvin in heat 13 and then with Louis in the very next heat for back-to-back 5-1s and Hackney were virtually home and dry. Thomas finished with a tremendous 11 paid 12 from the reserve berth.

The Hackney bandwagon rolled on with a win at home over Middlesbrough and it looked as though nothing could now prevent Hackney from certain championship victory. Controversy reigned at Long Eaton on 17 August when, due to a mixture of exclusions and engine failures, a match which should have seen an easy Hackney victory was surprisingly close and, with one heat to go, Long Eaton needed a 5-1 to draw. The tapes rose and the Invaders' Mike Spink and Darrell Branford sped into the lead. But on the third turn, Galvin drove hard underneath and both home riders fell. To the disgust of the home crowd, Branford was excluded. Later Galvin admitted: 'I did hit him. I dived for a hole because we needed a 5-1. Often we needed a 5-0 and that sort of thing happened a few times (laughs) I paid my way in fines but didn't care!' Hackney duly rode to their own 5-1 in the re-run and victory in the match 52-44. The atmosphere was fever pitch and one incensed Long Eaton fan climbed over the fence and threw a punch at Galvin.

A further away league victory at Middlesbrough on 25 August preceded the cup semi-final at Edinburgh the following night. The Kestrels emerged victorious 51-45 and followed up with a 71-25 hammering at Waterden road three nights later; the Kestrels were through to the cup final. Perhaps not surprisingly since they had beaten Hackney twice already, Poole had emerged as Hackney's nearest rivals for the championship. As the run-in commenced, the Kestrels were 10 points clear of the Pirates and Hackney were closing in on the championship. Loram returned to the side and came second in the National League Riders Championship at Coventry on 10 September. The following night, the Kestrels dropped only their fourth league point when they drew at Berwick. Interestingly, that result was arguably the best one for the Kestrels, as a draw meant that they could put the league beyond mathematical doubt and win the championship at their next home meeting, against Wimbledon.

Hackney beat the Dons 58-36 on 16 September and were league champions for the first time since 1938. A battle of words had existed throughout the year between the two London clubs and the visitors section of the programme simply said, 'This is what we think about them', a blank page lay underneath simply emblazoned at the bottom with 'Not a lot'. Barry Thomas celebrated by coming out for his last ride with balloons tied to his bike and the atmosphere was electric from the off. The success-starved Hackney fans at last had something to really cheer about. The applause rang out along with Queen's 'We are the Champions', as the Hackney team ran around the whole track showing off the trophy. The cup final was still to be fought, although this would be an all-London affair against Wimbledon.

The first leg was held at Waterden Road on 7 October, Hackney building a comfortable 24-point lead to take to Plough Lane. Before that, however, Hackney entered the record books for dropping the least amount of league points in a season. The record had been held by Newcastle, but the Kestrels broke it by beating Edinburgh home and away, finishing the campaign having scored 54 points and only having dropped six points – despite a late defeat at Stoke.

Having clinched the league at home to Wimbledon, fittingly the cup was secured at Plough Lane. The second leg was held on 19 October and Wimbledon promoter Russell Lanning offered begrudging congratulations in his programme notes, sadly wallowing in past Wimbledon triumphs in an obvious attempt to defuse the Hackney success story. It mattered not though, as Hackney led throughout and secured another victory on the night 50-46 and on aggregate 110-82 to complete the league and cup double for the first time in their history. If ever the Kestrels fans did not want a season to end it was this one. Not least of all as, amid all the celebrations, the dreaded points limit loomed and everybody knew when Hackney won late-season challenge matches both home and away against Eastbourne that it would be the last time the team ever rode together.

What a season it had been. In what had been a true team effort it was difficult to single out riders for praise. Loram, in only his second-ever season, and Galvin, who had revelled in the captaincy, were without doubt two of the best riders in the league, scoring magnificently almost everywhere. Galvin also won the reinstated London Riders Championship. Louis was the find of the season and in fact his scoring had made all the difference. Mogridge and Whittaker had ups and downs, but were there as very able back up and, on more than one occasion, saved the day – as did the veteran Thomas who, despite finding points harder to come by, was still a tremendous asset to the side. Gary Rolls had also more than played his part.

A special mention should be made of the team manager, John Louis. His inspirational guidance and tactical awareness turned many matches Hackney's way and his part in the success should not be underestimated. Ironically, he was soon to be seen as the villain of the break-up of the best ever National League side.

1988 National League Record (1/16 teams)

Played	Won	Drawn	Lost	For	Against	Pts
30	26	2	2	1,682	1,192	54

1988 Cup Record

Round 1	Poole	Won 110-82
Round 2	Middlesbrough	Won 107-85
Semi-final	Edinburgh	Won 122-70
Final	Wimbledon	Won 110-82

1988 National League and Cup Averages (captain in italics)

Rider	Mts	Rds	Pts	BP	Total	CMA	Maxs
Mark Loram	33	166	410	19	429	10.34	11
Andy Galvin	*37*	*193*	*426*	*50*	*476*	*9.87*	*7*
Chris Louis	38	182	333	33	366	8.04	2
Alan Mogridge	38	189	301	49	350	7.41	2
Paul Whittaker	38	185	283	54	337	7.29	4
Gary Rolls	36	126	160	27	187	5.94	
Barry Thomas	35	152	189	36	225	5.92	1

HACKNEY HERO

MARK LORAM

Hackney's World Champion

Early Loramski.

No Hackney rider ever won the World Championship whilst riding for Hackney. Both Jansson and Plech came close, but Hackney fans will claim a stake in the victory of World Champion 2000, Mark Loram. Mark started his career at Hackney as a sixteen-year-old in 1987, making the surprise decision to step straight into the British League. It was obvious that he was of the same mould of many riders that Hackney thrived upon over the years - a thrill-maker who brought people through the turnstiles. 'Dave Pavitt was the promoter and he was good friend of my dad's and he basically talked me into it. I was very close to joining Canterbury, but that year there was a rule that every team had to bring in a junior at number seven. Hackney had me and it worked out quite well, because the idea was that every meeting I was to go and try to beat my respective junior. Malcolm Simmons had been a great help throughout my career: from about the age of fourteen he helped me and was nothing but good for me. And Simon Wigg too, I always looked up to him and he brought me along as well. Simon was a true professional and it's strange that people (Hackney fans) did not take to him at that time.'

Although that year was a disaster for Hackney, Mark quickly established himself. Why then did he step down a league when Hackney returned to the National League the following year? 'They kinda said, "you've done ever so well but..." and again they wrapped me round their little finger and I was at the age where I was open to all sorts of ideas, but I don't regret it because it did what it was supposed to do and gave me a load of confidence. I went back up two years later when the time was right and avoided getting stale as some riders do.'

That year Hackney won everything in sight and Mark was a revelation, scoring over 10 points a match. Many people thought the atmosphere in the National League to be far superior to that of its senior counterpart. 'Andy [Galvin] was flying as well as myself and it was the year that Chris [Louis] shone through. Basically, Chris came with me to a few meetings in 1987. He was working in a garage as a panel beater and he fancied a go at it. The progress he made was quite outstanding. Despite my progress, it was a real team effort throughout.

When I was fifteen, I travelled around the country a lot as their mascot and, although some teams would not let me ride, I helped out a lot of the boys and it was so much fun from start to finish. There were always harmless punch ups which in those days all seemed part of it. I remember it as free-for-all, like a western half the time and for me growing up as a youngster, it's something I'll always remember; it's something that really is missing from speedway because that sort of thing doesn't happen very often. It was always so light-hearted and after it had happened it was never a problem. Obviously, Andy was a real fiery character and I quite often argued his corner in the pits. The Hackney track had a bit of a jaded history of injuries there, but that aside it was fun track to ride because of the shape of it. One of the guys I used to love watching ride round there was Barry Thomas because of the way he used to ride it. He was a model National League rider in them days; he was laid back and it's a wonder that he didn't go further than he did. He was such a nice guy. You need characters like that and we had fun right through the team.'

Why as a racer did Mark leave a renowned racetrack to go to Ipswich – which did not have the same reputation for passing. 'Again it was a funny one that, because although I moved to Ipswich it was run under the same banner and I did not look at it as a move. What went on behind the scenes with my contract I knew very little about. As far as I was concerned, I was a Hackney rider but more of a Dave Pavitt rider – I was offered the move to Ipswich and again I was kind of talked into it. I saw it as riding for a sister track.'

I remind Mark that the Hackney fans never saw it that way. 'No that's right, but it was more the promotion at the time's decision rather than mine. The fans were always great though.' What about the new Grand Prix circuit? 'It wasn't the old Waterden Road and it was a shame they never had the banking. It was a stadium with a track in, whereas before it was THE track with what you could call a stadium round it. The important thing was the stage and, unfortunately, when it was rebuilt that no longer became the most important bit – but having said that I think the track towards the end did produce some good racing, but of course when it was opened everything was rushed.'

After Ipswich, Mark went on to ride for King's Lynn, Exeter, Bradford, Poole, Peterborough and Eastbourne. Having won Grand Prixs in 1997 in Denmark and 1999 in Sweden he joined the rare band of English World Speedway Champions in 2000 and was the first to win under the new Grand Prix format. 'You always hope and dream and sometimes you think its never gonna happen, but some reason in the year 2000 I had a little bit of luck and it all seemed to come together. I could not put my finger on what, but I felt that I had been repaid for all the hard work. I could not single out any one person or any one time, but for sure the start I had played an important part. For me, Hackney was where I learned my trade – Saturday afternoons practicing there and then going into the team and riding there for two years. It really was a great part of the learning curve for me.'

1989 – The Calm After The Storm

During the opening months of the close season, Ipswich boss Chris Shears, ironically the man who had almost become Hackney promoter, was told that he would not have his lease renewed at Foxhall Heath. The Hackney Consortium felt that with John Louis being a legend in Ipswich, it would make good business sense to promote at both venues, which might give financial stability to both clubs. It would also solve the problems regarding the points limit.

The Hackney public did not see it that way, especially when they learned that the next piece of the masterplan involved taking Loram, Louis and (to a lesser extent) Mogridge to Foxhall Heath. John Louis and Mike Western would run Ipswich, whilst the remainder of the consortium would run Hackney. Many people thought Hackney had been sold out and Louis – who seemed desperate to get back to his beloved Ipswich – took the brunt of the blame. With three of the top four riders gone, the fans were placated somewhat when Hackney signed Steve Schofield from Poole. Born on 27 February 1958, Schofield had been an excellent and tenuous rider over the years, having commenced his career at Weymouth in 1983 and having seen British League service with Wolverhampton. He was undoubtedly the star of the National League, having finished 1988 top of the league averages, beating Loram into second place. He was also an accomplished grass-track and long-track rider. There was little doubt that Schofield and Galvin would make as formidable a spearhead as Galvin and Loram had done, but it was the back-up where most of the worries lay. Whittaker and Rolls had been retained and into the reserve berths came youngsters Lee Pavitt and, on loan from Reading, Gary Tagg. Completing the line-up and celebrating twenty years at Hackney was Barry Thomas.

Again the league campaign got off to an early start and Glasgow were thrashed 62-33 on 31 March. Wimbledon followed in the London Pride challenge match seven days later and managed to restrict the Kestrels to a draw. The real action was saved up for the return at Plough Lane on 12 April, this time Hackney emerging victorious 48-47, having scored a 5-0 in the last race – enabling Hackney to proudly boasted that they had not lost to Wimbledon since July 1986. Hackney's away league matches commenced at Rye House four days after the Wimbledon match and, with yet more drama, they won the match by scoring another last heat 5-0!

The first Northern tour was scheduled for 28 and 29 of April and, as usual, these matches would always provide an indication as to the chances of league success. Hackney were well beaten in both matches and lost Gary Rolls at Berwick with a broken thumb. May saw qualification for the four-team championship, but Poole gained revenge for the previous season by knocking Hackney out of the cup. Further heavy away defeats followed, and it was hard to deny that Hackney were pretty much a two-man team. Lee Pavitt had found the going a little tough and had been replaced by Michael Warren.

Tragedy was to strike yet again on 30 June when Arena Essex visited in the second leg of the LonEx (London-Essex) Trophy. With both Galvin and Warren injured, twenty-three-year-old junior Paul Muchene was drafted in to make his debut for the Kestrels.

He led heat 2 but fell on the pits bend and was struck by Hammers reserve Nick Floyd, who could not avoid him. Muchene was rushed to hospital and placed on a life support machine but died the following Tuesday at St Bartholomew's Hospital.

Hackney's chances of success in the four-team final were crushed when Schofield missed the event at Peterborough because he was riding in the World Long-track semi-final. Without him, Hackney could only manage 5 points in their semi-final and, to add insult to injury, Schofield's qualification for the long-track final ruled him out of the National League Pairs too. The clash that everyone was waiting for, against Ipswich, was held on 4 August. Fortunately for the consortium, Hackney swept the Witches aside, winning 51-44. Predictably, Loram and Louis put up most resistance, but both were upstaged by Schofield who scored a 15-point maximum. The National League Best Pairs was held on 19 August and Hackney, represented by Galvin and Whittaker, were still unable to capitalise on home advantage and went out of it in the semi-final to Mildenhall.

Hackney finished in sixth place, which after the previous season was a disappointment. Schofield was immaculate throughout and was again top of the averages, both for Hackney and the entire league. He scored 10 in the NLRC and his 15-point maximum in the last home match against Poole on 13 October was his eighth successive home league maximum. Galvin was second in the league averages, giving the fans the pleasure of the Hackney's top two outscoring Ipswich's Loram and Louis. Whittaker, now twenty-one and in his sixth season, had become a solid second string but had still failed to realise the potential he had shown on joining the team as a

Steve Schofield.

sixteen-year-old. Tagg and Rolls had battled gamely and Warren had shown one or two glimpses of potential.

As the season came to a close, speculation turned to Thomas and what he would do after his testimonial meeting. It was true that he was finding points harder and harder to come by, but as usual there was always the odd glittering performance. One such occasion came in Hackney's last competitive match of the campaign, just a week before the testimonial. Wimbledon visited in the second leg of the London Cup just 2 points in front. It was a vintage Thomas display and his 9 paid 10 helped ensure that Hackney's season finished with victory in a competition that was still very important to the two clubs concerned.

1989 National League Record (6/18 teams)

Played	Won	Drawn	Lost	For	Against	Pts
34	19	1	14	1,701	1,557	39

1989 Cup Record

Round 1	Bye	
Round 2	Poole	Lost 75-117

1989 National League and Cup Averages (captain in italics)

Rider	Mts	Rds	Pts	BP	Total	CMA	Maxs
Steve Schofield	36	192	491	13	504	10.50	12
Andy Galvin	*36*	*193*	*463*	*17*	*480*	*9.95*	*9*
Paul Whittaker	36	182	292	34	326	7.17	
Gary Tagg	34	166	184	39	223	5.37	
Barry Thomas	36	164	154	24	178	4.34	
Gary Rolls	14	57	49	10	59	4.14	
Michael Warren	28	108	80	14	94	3.48	
Lee Pavitt	13	37	24	5	29	3.14	

HACKNEY HERO

BARRY THOMAS

Blood, Sweat and Beers

For many people Barry Thomas was Hackney Speedway. 'Thommo', as he was affectionately known to his fans, was born in Harrow, Middlesex on 29 October 1951. At the age of ten he got his first bike, an Excelsior 197, and four years later he joined the Kent Youth Grass-track Association. Barry and Dave Jessup stood out from the crowd and were invited to second-half trials at West Ham and Barry was soon offered a contract with Canterbury. Aboard his first proper speedway bike, a £95 Jap, he progressed from second halves into the Canterbury team and finished the 1969 season as one of their heat leaders.

During that season he made his first appearance at Hackney, scoring 1 point in the Autumn Extra Trophy on 31 October 1969. Geoff Maloney thus became the very first rider to be beaten by Thommo at Waterden Road. In 1970, Thommo joined Hackney and later that season he won his first major individual title at Swindon by becoming the Junior Champion of the British Isles. 'Len was down at Canterbury with Rayleigh and he approached me and asked if I wanted a second-half ride at Hackney. You could learn a lot from Banger by just watching what he did on the track, but I would say that the person that went out of his way to help me was Middleton. He used to put me up at his place and, if I had bike trouble, he used to help me sort it out. He did a special fuel mix for the British Junior Championship with nitro in it and he organised some Continental trips for me. He was a bit of a character.'

'I actually had a part in Zenon coming to England. I'd raced him at Hackney when I rode for England and we had a couple of good races. Later on in Poland I was chatting to him. It was the first time I had really spoken to him and I said to him, "How would you feel about coming to ride for Hackney?" Zenon said he fancied it and when I came back I went into Len's office and told him that Zenon would be prepared to ride for him. I said just contact him and Len did. Len always got the credit for it.'

Among the riding highlights were international caps for his country and two victories in the London Rider Championship. He was also Hackney captain for nine of his twenty seasons. 'I never expected to become captain and I took it seriously, but Len understood that after the meeting I wanted to mingle with the supporters and have a beer. But the modern promoters didn't see that side of it and I clashed a little with them 'cos I wanted to carry on the old way and they wanted the super professional approach. The supporters liked seeing the riders and having a chat, but now the riders just go home.'

Who said Thommo couldn't gate? Here he is clearly going to make the drop on Steve Bastable.

Although he never qualified for a World Final he beat many World Champions – his crowning moment coming when he beat Ivan Mauger in 1977. 'I had been following them for three laps and I was trying to line myself up to get Mauger on the inside, but I realised that wasn't going to come off. Mauger went into the last turn tighter and Autry came off the entry to the corner further into mid-track. That left a gap on the outside and I knew there was some dirt there and it was a last-ditch effort. I just had to try something and it paid off. People remember it but I tell people my throttle jammed!'

As the rider that knew the track the best how did he rate it against its safety record? 'It was one of the best racing tracks and I loved it because, not being a good gater, I always had a chance from the back. I wouldn't like to say it was 100 per cent safe as it had a bad record. I was lucky to hit the right part of the fence when I crashed. It was the lamp-posts – but it was not the only track with poles around it. As captain, I had to fill in forms for the SRA at every track I went to and I spotted several dangers. Len did a lot to improve the safety. A lot of it's luck and I was lucky enough to always walk away. I've always said that I think it was more dangerous driving to the meetings. In 1970 I did 80,000 miles in nine months – that's got to make it more likely that you'll get killed on the road, especially the way we all drove!'

After eleven seasons, Thommo decided to move on to Crayford: 'I was struggling a little bit and was getting a bit stale. It was good for my confidence and I think it worked. When I came back as number eight I did okay. I got my head right and the bike going good and when I came back to Hackney I had confidence. I think it was a bit embarrassing for Len, because he felt he had to put me in and at the same time felt he had to put Bob Garrad in as he was up and coming.'

When Crayford closed, he found himself back at the Wick, where he would pass on invaluable experience and knowledge to Hackney's younger riders. Latter-day Hackney stars, including Galvin and Loram, all benefited hugely from riding in the same team as Thommo and many others were coached during the years he ran training schools at the Iwade circuit that he built himself. 'I always felt that Hackney was my place and it felt like coming home for me. It was great to see the boys going so well.'

But Thommo never fulfilled the potential he had. He was also inconsistent, being beaten by a complete novice in one race and then coming out and beating the opposition's number one by a mile in the next. Does Thommo regret not getting better results? 'I have thought about it quite often and if I could do it all again, I might try a more professional approach, but then I may have fizzled out after ten years. It's a nagging doubt. What if I had lived and breathed speedway 100% all the time. There was lots of pressure involved and I wanted to relax at the end of it, although I overdid it a bit to say the least (laughs).'

There were Hackney riders that scored more points, but Thommo's style and the design of the Hackney circuit were made for each other. The steep banking and Thommo's breathtaking ability to blast around the outside right on the kick boards made for the most exciting action ever seen at Waterden Road. Thommo was a thrill merchant and a crowd-puller – something that was still evident during his one-off comeback at Rye House in 2001, to date his last appearance for Hackney. 'I found it a bit weird because I had not had any chance to practice. The first thing that hit me was how fast it was. Whereas when you're doing it all the time you're never going fast enough. But having been away from it so long, I was pleased I was keeping up with them. By the third race I was just getting into it.'

When Thommo and I worked together as rider and sponsor he was quite simply what many people had said and written before, a lovely bloke. The best tribute that can possibly be paid is that Barry Thomas thrilled and entertained people all over the country and, on a regular basis, turned an average match into a thriller by giving Hackney fans the time of their lives. In Len Silver's words: 'speedway may never see his like again'.

The Thommo Testimonials
1979 and 1989

On 4 November 1979 Barry Thomas celebrated his first ten years as a Hackney rider. Ten years later on 2 November 1989, Thomas made speedway history by becoming the first rider to complete twenty seasons with the same club and be honoured with a double testimonial. A unique achievement – and a record that still stands today. 'Is that still a record? I don't know where the time went. People would joke that I was heading for my second one and then there it was. I might come back and do another ten years when they re-open. Please thank everyone who supported me through all those years.'

His first meeting saw the 1979 Hackney team take on a Kent select side. Barry had lived for many years in Kent and that county had produced many of 1979's top talent – including three former World Finalists, Malcolm Simmons, Gordon Kennett and Dave Jessup, all three of whom were old mates of Thommo. The remainder of the side was made up of old team-mates Barney Kennett, Laurie Etheridge and the recently retired Bobby McNeil, as well as Oxford's Les Rumsey. Needless to say this was quite a competitive team and it was not surprising that Kent raced to a 9-point lead. But the Hawks hit back with Plech and Thomas in fine form and Hackney emerged with the narrowest of victories, 39-38. After the main event, Thommo gave the crowd a display of leg-trailing, following his thrilling display in the previous year's Golden Jubilee meeting – this time competing in a match race with paralysed ex-Hackney rider Graham Miles, who drove a specially modified go-kart.

The second half was billed as the Barry Thomas Testimonial Trophy. Simmons, Jessup, Petersen and Thomas were the riders that reached the final and, unbeknown to Barry, the others had agreed to let him win the trophy. Typically of Thommo, he fell in an attempt to drive round them and Petersen rode on to win.

Hackney 39:
Plech 9, Thomas 8, Thomsen 6, Petersen 5, White 5, Willmott 4, Odermatt 2

Kent 38:
Jessup 9, Simmons 8, G Kennett 8, B Kennett 5, Rumsey 4, Etheridge 3, McNeil 1

Barry's second testimonial was originally going to be on 29 October, but terrible weather forced the meeting to be postponed and re-arranged for the following Friday. Sadly, this was to mean that ex-Hackney star Bengt Jansson would not be able to appear. Another Hackney legend did ride though. Zenon Plech made two appearances, including a match race against former World Champion Peter Collins, which ended in a dead heat.

The main event was a four-team tournament, which saw the Kestrels take on Razzers Rockets (Jens Rasmussen), Bucks Fizzers (Andy Buck) and Bo's Buccaneers (Bo Petersen). Petersen, still a major force around Waterden road six years after he left Hackney, scored a faultless 12-point maximum. Joining him from the first testimonial meeting was Gordon Kennett and, a late inclusion after the rain-off was a team-mate

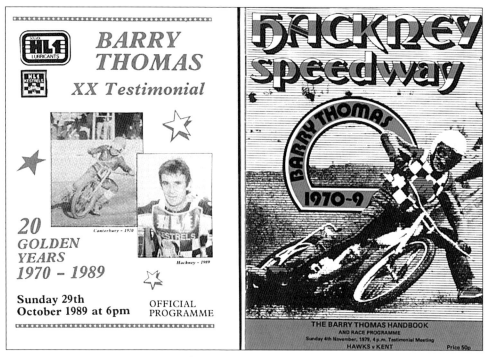

Programmes from Barry Thomas's testimonial.

from 1989, Steve Schofield. This made for an impressive line-up, but the Kestrels team – made up of Thommo and three riders he had coached during their formative years, Andy Galvin, Alan Mogridge and Paul Whittaker – poetically stole victory by a single point.

Kestrels 29:
Galvin 10, Thomas 7, Mogridge 7, Whittaker 5

Buccaneers 28:
Petersen 12, Schofield 10, Kennett 3, Andy Hines 3

Fizzers 20:
Les Collins 8, Buck 6, Michael Coles 3, Michael Warren 3, Martin Goodwin 0

Rockets 19:
Rasmussen 6, Peter Glanz 6, Mel Taylor 5, Kelvin Mullarkey 2

5

THE WICK DIES
1990-96

1990 – Storm Clouds Gather

Perhaps not surprisingly, Barry Thomas decided to retire after a lifetime's service at Hackney. He would be missed, especially at home meetings. Bravely, the promotion opened the season with home-and-away challenge matches featuring both their teams. Both won their home matches, but Ipswich triumphed on aggregate. Andy Galvin and Steve Schofield were expected to pick up their dramatic scoring where they left off. Paul Whittaker, Gary Tagg and Michael Warren had all done enough to be retained and, with the National League now open to foreign riders, they were joined by twenty-one-year-old Dane Tim Korneliussen and Aussie Dave Hamnett.

Many people were surprised that there had been no established signing to bolster the team, but a double win in the first Northern Tour (at Berwick 47-46 and Edinburgh 56-40) had people sitting up and taking notice. Korneliussen had started like a train and Warren was scoring well in the difficult number two berth. These two were providing good backing to Galvin, Schofield and Whittaker. Added to these victories were two home wins and Hackney, perhaps against everyone's expectations, were unbeaten at the end of April with four wins.

4 May brought Long Eaton to town and, for the first time ever, a rider completed four laps at Waterden Road in under a minute. Andy Galvin broke Erik Gundersen's three-year-old track record and the minute barrier by recording a time of 59.5 seconds. Another record fell that night when Schofield was beaten for the first time at home in 51 league races as his clutch burned out and he failed to score in his first ride. Korneliussen was soon ruled out though with food poisoning, but that did not prevent more wins, this time at Stoke 49-47 and Exeter 51-45, and also at home against Newcastle.

Despite two away defeats at Wimbledon and Peterborough, Hackney was doing well in the league and had won again at Milton Keynes. They had qualified for the finals of the four-team championship and progressed to the next round of the cup with home and away wins over Eastbourne. And as if that was not enough, the first silverware had been secured when, after many near misses in the past, Hackney managed to win the National League Best Pairs at Glasgow through Galvin and Schofield, who beat Exeter in the final.

Sadly, the season was about to turn and it was to be all downhill after that in more ways than one. The Kestrels began to lose their way with a defeat at Long Eaton.

Tim Korneliussen.

Perhaps the major reason was the loss of form of Korneliussen, who following the food poisoning bout was struggling after a bad crash at Wimbledon. On 3 August, the night of Peterborough's visit, Dave Pavitt announced that the day-to-day running of the club was to be taken over new director Derek Howes. Pavitt claimed pressure of business but, rightly or wrongly, many saw this as the next move in the long-term plan to dump Hackney for Ipswich. It was to have dire consequences for Hackney Speedway.

Hackney lost at Ipswich by a solitary point after Steve Schofield was strangely excluded after Shane Parker fell in heat 15, although amidst the gloom the Kestrels managed to finish third in the final of the four-team tournament on 5 August. Poole knocked the Kestrels out of the cup, winning both legs, and just three weeks later on 31 August won at Waterden Road again, this time in the league. The season was to really crumble on 2 September during the Kestrels' away match at Rye House. Heat 5 saw Galvin line up with Korneliussen against Glen Baxter and Scott Humphries. Baxter shot into the lead with Korneliussen second and Humphries third. Along the back straight, Galvin moved into third place: 'Scott Humphries hit me. I missed the start and overtook Scott. But I cut back to cut underneath another and he lifted. It wasn't his fault, he hit a rut and T-boned me. There was only one post round the whole track and I hit it.' Galvin sustained a triple break of the right thigh. Hackney lost 46-50 and Galvin would never ride for Hackney again.

Not surprisingly, the Kestrels lost their first home match without Galvin to Arena Essex 44-50, with luck truly deserting them. Schofield fell in his first race and, although he won his next two races, he eventually was forced to withdraw from the meeting with a back injury. To complete a miserable September, Korneliussen broke his thigh away at Glasgow on 26 September and, two nights later, Schofield was ruled out with a knee injury – causing him to miss what little remained of the season.

With the loss of the top two, Paul Whittaker had been quietly scoring better and better and revelling in his newfound responsibility as stand-in skipper. A magnificent 20-point haul at Newcastle ensured there was a final victory to cheer and his final average was his best ever in a Hackney race-jacket. Schofield was excellent again and just missed out on a third successive year at the top of the National League Averages; he scored 9 in the BLRC. Tagg, after a disastrous start, showed he did indeed have the potential to go further and Warren too had improved and scored consistently. Korneliussen had looked a world beater but in the end, not helped by injury, he was a disappointment and Hamnett had been enigmatic throughout.

Galvin had been a tremendous rider for the club. Having joined as a young inexperienced rider from Crayford, he became one of the National League's top performers, feared no one and was a real mixer. He had played significant roles in Hackney's successes since joining the National League and had probably harmed his own career by not moving into the British League and staying at the Wick instead. Fifth place was again a more-than-respectable position, but after the early season victories had to be viewed as a disappointment – although after several near misses Hackney did at last get their name on the Best Pairs trophy. As the winter set in the Hackney fans were perhaps bemoaning the bad luck that had wrecked the season, but nothing could have prepared them for what lay ahead.

1990 National League Record (5/18 teams)

Played	Won	Drawn	Lost	For	Against	Pts
32	19	0	13	1,608	1,451	38

1990 Cup Record

Round 1	Bye	
Round 2	Eastbourne	Won 170-72
Round 3	Poole	Lost 80-110

1990 National League and Cup Averages (captain in italics)

Rider	Mts	Rds	Pts	BP	Total	CMA	Maxs
Steve Schofield	34	180	467	6	473	10.51	10
Andy Galvin	27	132	279	27	306	9.27	6
Paul Whittaker	36	199	390	17	407	8.18	2
Gary Tagg	32	159	193	44	237	5.96	
Michael Warren	36	188	222	34	256	5.45	
Dave Hamnett	32	117	114	15	129	4.41	
Tim Korneliussen	27	100	88	11	99	3.96	
Shawn Venables	9	40	30	8	38	3.80	

HACKNEY HERO

ANDY GALVIN

5-0 Required!

Andy Galvin first rode for Crayford in 1982 when just sixteen years old, having commenced his career at Iwade under the watchful eye of his mentor Barry Thomas. Early in his career, Thommo put him through his crash course... 'We were at Crayford and Terry Russell decided we would have gating practice at Iwade. I was team riding alongside Thommo, but he shoved me out and knocked me off and I broke my wrist! I'd only just come back from a broken ankle.'

After another season at Crayford the club closed and Andy moved to Hackney for 1984. 'I didn't like Hackney at first, it seemed so big with the big banking. It was an eye-opener for someone so young and going for it. Riders used to think they were wide but we always went wider and overtook them – it was hair-raising though.' After three seasons gradually improving at the Wick, Andy stepped up to the British League with the Kestrels in 1987 and his potential really started to show: 'Wiggy was always bubbly and professional and that opened my eyes to many things. Simmo was exceptional for his age and I learnt a lot about the workshop from him.'

The following year, Andy was made captain and under his leadership Hackney swept all before them. How did he view that team? 'We had a team coach and went everywhere together. The team spirit was brilliant. I loved being captain, running up and down the pits like a looney getting everyone geed up. Chris Louis was my partner and I got him off to a good start. He could gate like anything, team riding and making gaps for each other – a great combination which produced many 5-1s. Paul Whittaker was a points machine: he always got his 7 or 9. Mark Loram has done so well. We went to the same school, although I am older. I was so pleased for him when he became World Champion.'

Which rider was Andy's biggest influence? 'In my early days I looked up to Thommo. He was absolutely the worst gater in the world but that's why he was an excellent racer, with his big swoops around the outside. I would trust him with my life – he was my hero. He was a natural; he could stay up all night drinking and then go out and score a maximum the next night. He could have been square like Dave Jessup and take sandwiches and a flask everywhere (laughs). Once Thommo fitted a new engine into his bike on the coach. We were travelling along and the coach had a little workshop in the back. The next minute he fired it up and revved it like anything. It filled the coach up with black smoke and we had to evacuate the coach on the hard shoulder.'

In 1990 Andy broke his thigh at Rye House, which finished his Hackney career. Does he regret going to Arena Essex since it may have been better to come back from such a serious injury at a track he knew? 'Arena never really suited me but I enjoyed it there – but I needed more of a racers' track and it was tight and therefore hard on turning, especially my right leg which I broke. My leg was fine but then I had the big one and hurt by back and neck and that put paid to that for eight or nine years. The way Mark [Loram] and Chris [Louis] went, I think I could have gone all the way but you can never tell.'

Andy was due to make one last appearance for Hackney at Rye House in 2001. 'I was disappointed not to be able to ride, just because my average was 0.01 too high. Ridiculous, and it's the fans that suffer – typical speedway. I wanted to ride again with Thommo and I heard he went alright – still elbows everywhere! My glory days were definitely at Hackney. I was scoring good points and the crowd loved us. I wouldn't do anything different. But I owe a lot to Terry (Russell).'

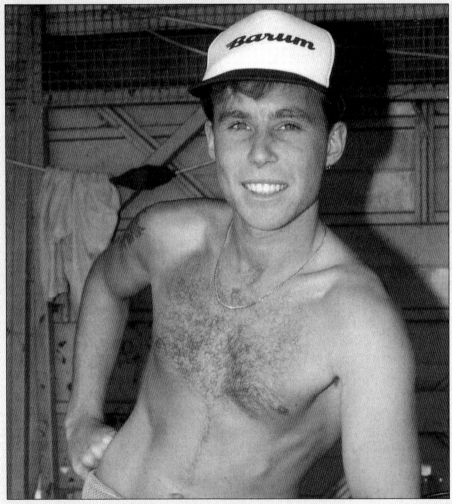

Andy Galvin – a hit with the Hackney females!

1991 – The End In The East

During the close season, it was clear that Pavitt's role was going to be non-existent (despite being billed in the programme as consultant promoter) and that Derek Howes was effectively on his own. During the winter the leagues had been renamed, British League Division One and Two, and Howes' first act was to change the name of the team back to make them Hackney Hawks for the first time since 1983. An almost completely new line-up was to take to the track. Another former Hackney promoter, Terry Russell, had returned to the sport in charge at Arena Essex and had taken his long-term protégé Andy Galvin with him. Steve Schofield was gone, having returned to Poole. Both Galvin and Schofield would be very hard to replace. Paul Whittaker was to lead the Hawks, having been made the new captain, but the team's number one would be Swede Tony Olsson, who had ridden in the World Final in 1989 and had been signed on loan from Reading. Michael Warren and Dave Hamnett both lined up again, but to complete the squad Hackney turned to unknown foreign riders: Tim Hunter, a young Aussie, and unknown Czech Pavel Karnas. Junior Roland Pollard completed the side.

The season had hardly commenced when the events of 12 March first sounded the death knell. As with many tracks, crowds at Hackney had been visibly falling as speedway plunged further into decline. That night the World Championship qualifier was held and a large crowd had assembled to see a comeback attempt by former World Champion Michael Lee. Five heats had been completed when suddenly most of the

Paul Whittaker.

lights around the track and in the pits area went out. The meeting was abandoned but, worse still, when the lights came back on, the night's admission takings were gone and with them any hope that Hackney would survive the current speedway downturn.

Tim Hunter had struggled and he lost his team place to a Czech, Vladimir Kalina, after the Hawks lost narrowly away at Rye House and Arena Essex. At home it looked as though the team could and would hold its own, including a superb performance in thumping Rye House 52-37, with a disgruntled Martin Goodwin smashing the referee box window with his crash helmet having been excluded from heat 12. 17 May brought Arena Essex and its array of former Hackney riders back to Waterden Road. Although Galvin looked a shadow of his former self, Petersen looked every bit the classy rider he was when riding for the Hawks in the 1970s and '80s. His 10 points, combined with 13 from Mogridge, helped the Hammers to a 10-point win.

As June commenced, Wimbledon finally succumbed after many years of staving off closure, leaving Hackney the only club left in the capital – but not for long. Arena Essex returned on 14 June, this time for a league match, and, despite a repeat good performance by Petersen and Mogridge, Whittaker was the star of the night, racing to 13 points. Hackney emerged victorious 47-42. However, apart from Whittaker and Olssen, the rest of the team were struggling, although Warren and Hamnett were battling hard with some success.

A barren spell followed, despite Hackney signing veteran Swede Richard Hellsen in an attempt to bolster the team. What was perhaps the final straw came at Newcastle on 30 June. Only 6 points separated the teams after twelve heats of the cup match when in heat 13 Paul Whittaker crashed and broke his arm. As the week preceding the return tie with Newcastle commenced, rumours were flying that Hackney were in serious financial trouble and on the evening prior to the match it was reported that the following night's meeting may be the last at Waterden Road unless a sponsor or financial backer came forward to save the club. There was no mention of difficulties in that night's programme, but the crowd were subdued and feared the worst. Hackney emerged victorious, beating Newcastle 46-44 after a last heat 5-1 by Olssen and Hamnett. It was the last meeting ever to be held on Hackney's renowned banked Waterden Road track and, later that week, the fans' worst fears were confirmed and closure was announced, ending a run of twenty-nine consecutive years.

As the season carried on there was no sign of any interest in re-opening the track – which had after all been in decline every since that magnificent season of 1988. The state of speedway in general, the loss of exciting riders Thomas, Galvin and Schofield, and the perceived sell-out by Louis and Pavitt were probably all contributing factors. Sadly, like so many great venues before them, Hackney was consigned to the history books. In this case, undoubtedly the biggest tragedy was the loss of one of the fairest and most exciting racing tracks there had ever been. It was not quite over yet though.

1991 British League Division Two

Expunged

1991 Cup Record

Round 1	Bye	
Round 2	Newcastle	Lost 84-96

1991 League, Gold Cup and Cup Averages (captain in italics)

Expunged, guidance only

Rider	Mts	Rds	Pts	BP	Total	CMA	Maxs
Paul Whittaker	*19*	*98*	*198*	*11*	*209*	*8.53*	*2*
Tony Olsson	20	103	197	7	204	7.92	1
Dave Hamnett	18	99	157	14	171	6.91	
Vladimir Kalina	14	59	70	16	86	5.83	
Michael Warren	22	100	121	13	134	5.36	
Rickard Hellsen	7	32	40	1	41	5.13	
Pavel Karnas	16	58	55	12	67	4.62	
Roland Pollard	14	43	31	5	36	3.35	
Tim Hunter	13	46	21	5	26	2.26	

1995 – Grand Prix

During the course of 1994, the original Hackney stadium was demolished after sixty-two years of service. The old stadium was looking its age, but many lamented the loss of one of the last of the atmospheric old London stadia. Controversially, the old one-off World Finals had been scrapped and replaced with a Formula One-type Grand Prix system. The inaugural series was run over six rounds, with the British Grand Prix being the final round. Riders competed over the traditional twenty-heat individual formula and then competed in D, C, B and A, finals depending on where a rider finished in the main meeting. The finishing position in these finals determined the amount of Grand Prix points scored. A major London venue was required and the new Hackney stadium was chosen to host the 1995 British Grand Prix.

The track was completely new and, although the banking was gone, it was hoped that the racing would still be as exciting as it had once been. The new main stand that had been erected was impressive in appearance. Although not to everyone's liking, the stadium was full and the atmosphere was electric as, after a four-year absence speedway returned to Hackney on 30 September 1995, with what was effectively the World Final. Although it was not Wembley by a long way, it was still the biggest thing speedway had seen in the UK since the 1981 World Final.

Ominously for Hackney, former World Champion Barry Briggs commentating for Sky Sports described how the old circuit had banking and smooth corners whilst the new

Speedway returns to the Wick. There is a new stadium with only the listed tote board still standing.

track had corners that came to an apex and a reverse camber which would ensure that there was not much overtaking on the outside. He would be proved right in regard to the meeting and the track design was to play a crucial role in the future of Hackney.

Hans Nielsen was leading the field with 89 points from reigning World Champion Tony Rickardsen on 80. This lead meant that Nielsen only had to reach the B final to win his fourth World Championship final. To add a little more interest, former Hackney riders Mark Loram and Chris Louis were in the line-up, having become two of England's best riders in the years since they started their careers at the Wick.

Louis' meeting got off to a disastrous start when his cut-out came out as the tapes rose on heat 1. More drama unfolded in heat 3, where big guns Nielsen and Rickardsen met. Heavy rain had started to fall and Nielsen sped away from the tapes to lead but, entering the first bend on lap two, Nielsen spun and fell, giving Rickardsen a great opportunity to close the gap. However, that opportunity lasted less than a single lap in the re-run. Trailing Mark Loram, Rickardsen came into the third and fourth turns fast and close to the leader. He clipped the British rider's back wheel and fell. A broken collarbone was the result and, although he bravely carried on in order to secure second place in the final standings, it effectively handed the title to Nielsen.

Heat 14 saw Nielsen line up against Hamill, Michael Karlsson and the unbeaten Jason Crump. A win ensured that his score of 7 was enough to qualify for the B final and therefore was crowned as World Champion for the fourth time.

Grand Prix action.

However, there was a little more drama to come. In the C final Australian Craig Boyce overtook Poland's new superstar Tomasz Gollob coming done the home straight but, as they entered the first turn, Gollob dived up the inside then drifted out and into Boyce, taking him into the fence. Boyce walked back towards the starting gate and, as he came alongside Gollob, punched him with such force that Gollob fell off his bike. Both were excluded: Gollob for the crash and Boyce for the punch.

The A final was won by American Greg Hancock from his fellow countryman Sam Ermolenko. Old Hackney fans could be pleased that in third place was Mark Loram. At this early stage the Grand Prix series was on trial, with many lamenting the loss of the one-off final – but the sceptics were mostly won over and history went on to prove the Grand Prix a success. The meeting was not a classic, but held enough action and controversy to make it entertaining. The 11,000 people reported to be in attendance seemed to enjoy the occasion.

1996 – The London Lions

It was a disaster from the start. For many fans, the track was not THE TRACK, and hopes that it would prove anywhere near as good or even improve failed to materialise and it was exposed as a poor circuit. To add insult to injury, the back-straight stand, although open for the Grand Prix, was closed down as being apparently unsafe. As if this was not enough, there was nowhere to stand outside. The first and second turns were barren of any sort of stand and the third and fourth turns were simply a large mound of earth. Fans had to sit in the new impressive main stand which, having been designed for greyhound racing, was complexly enclosed by glass and to a large extent soundproof.

Promoters Terry Russell, Ivan Henry and Colin Pratt decided on a gamble and renamed the team the London Lions. Hackney's catchment area had changed dramatically over the years and, with no other London club likely to return, it was a gamble worth taking. Publicity for the London team may have been easier to come by and it may well have attracted people from Hackney's old rivals unwilling to support Hackney but willing to start with a fresh team called London.

On paper, the team that was assembled looked powerful. From Arena, Russell brought with him Australian star Leigh Adams, American international Josh Larsen, young British rider Paul Hurry and ex-Hackney star Alan Mogridge. To complement them, Kelvin Tatum was signed – rejoining a London side having commenced his career with Wimbledon. John Wainwright and the unknown youngster Dave Mason occupied the reserve berths.

In another change from the past, Thursday night would be the new racenight and so, on 28 March, league speedway returned to Waterden Road and the London Lions took on Peterborough in a challenge match. Although the track and stadium were not ideal, many old Hackney fans were present to see the rebirth. The racing was unspectacular but not boring and the Lions managed a 51-45 victory, Kelvin Tatum scoring an impressive 14 points.

Clearly fans were upset about the lack of outside viewing from the start, as an apology was made in the following week's programme and promises were made to fix the problem as soon as possible. That week Ipswich were entertained in the Premier League and, unlike days of old, were easily defeated 56-40 with maximums from Tatum and Leigh Adams. Twenty-four hours later and the Lions took the Witches to a last-heat decider. The requisite 5-1 was reversed and London had to be content with the bonus point for aggregate success.

On 15 May, London won at Poole, 51-45. Josh Larsen put in his best performance of the season with 12 points and new signing Neville Tatum, Kelvin's brother, scored 12 paid 13 from reserve. The younger Tatum had replaced Alan Mogridge, who had struggled from the off and, quite simply, could not get on with the London track. The Lions also defeated Reading in the cup, even without Leigh Adams – who had broken a collarbone in the Polish Grand Prix.

May concluded with the visit of the Scottish Monarchs. Colin Pratt's programme notes promised outside viewing would be available by the following week and the team was performing quite well, although the track was still taking time to settle down. Two heats had been completed when all power to the stadium was lost after an external power cut. Although darkness was not a problem, with no starting gate or track lights and with no air conditioning in the glass grandstand, the meeting was abandoned.

The London Riders Championship was held for the first time since 1988, but the grand old competition was hardly done any favours as it was contested by a line-up that was not world class, with many of the riders having no connection with London. Fortunately a world-class rider, Billy Hamill, was victorious.

The four-team tournament was held on 11 June, with five teams in London's group, each team participating in four of the five rounds. The Lions were missing Adams, Larsen and Kelvin Tatum, and the team of reserves scored a solitary 10 points on their home track, with Dane Jan Pedersen making his home debut, replacing the out-of-touch Dave Mason. The back-straight stand was still not open, but it was possible to stand on the steps directly in front. There was also a small standing area opened on the second bend. However, the racing and the crowds were not good, and it was an open secret that the stadium owners were in financial difficulty.

Peterborough dumped London out of the cup – the Lions' chances of victory having been hit with the loss of Jan Pedersen during a match at Hull two days before the second leg. Pedersen had been beginning to score a few points, but in heat 12 he crashed and cracked his hip, ruling him out for the remainder of the season. The British Grand Prix was another success, with Jason Crump winning the A final from Hans Nielsen, Billy Hamill and Greg Hancock. The biggest talking point was the rematch between last season's protagonists, Tomas Gollob and Craig Boyce. They did not disappoint and this time it was Boyce who knocked Gollob off in heat 17, earning him an exclusion. This time there was no fight.

Once the meeting was over, it was time to start facing up to the realities. The return of speedway to Waterden Road had not been a success and whilst the promoters kept quiet on the issue, the fans on the terraces were bracing themselves for the worst. John Wainwright joined the injury list, dislocating a shoulder at Oxford on 13 September, but the Lions won 53-43 and, on 3 October 1996, speedway was held at Waterden Road for the last time. Oxford were the visitors in London's last home league match and, perhaps fittingly, the meeting only lasted twelve heats before rain brought a sad and damp end to Hackney Speedway. The score, 40-32 to the Lions, was allowed to stand and perhaps nobody had the stomach to run another meeting. In their only season, the London Lions finished ninth out of 19. Leigh Adams was the star of the show and a world-class rider, finishing in fifteenth in the Grand Prix. Kelvin Tatum was still a force to be reckoned with, and both Paul Hurry and Neville Tatum had done quietly well. Josh Larsen was a little disappointing.

The promoters deserve credit for trying, but with a poor track and stadium facilities suiting greyhound racing and not speedway, the gamble did not pay off. Given time and better crowds, the Lions may have continued to find success, but in the end the stadium owners went bust. With them went the hopes of the long-term return of Hackney.

1996 Premier League Record (9/19 teams)

Played	Won	Drawn	Lost	For	Against	Pts
36	20	0	16	1732½	1693½	51

1996 Cup Record

Round 1	Bye	
Round 2	Reading	Won 110-82
Round 3	Peterborough	Lost 95-97

1996 Premier League and Cup Averages (captain in italics)

Rider	Mts	Rds	Pts	BP	Total	CMA	Maxs
Leigh Adams	*35*	*181*	*430*	*28*	*458*	*10.12*	*11*
Kelvin Tatum	32	160	348	18	366	9.15	4
Paul Hurry	26	126	224	10	234	7.43	1
Josh Larsen	35	174	273½	45	318½	7.32	1
Neville Tatum	25	126	166	26	192	6.10	
Jan Pedersen	11	41	39	7	46	4.49	
John Wainwright	32	124	83	28	111	3.58	
Alan Mogridge	11	46	34	6	40	3.48	
Dave Mason	23	77	27	7	34	1.77	

Hackney then – an atmospheric Thirties stadium.

Hackney now – a Millennium-neglected arena.

EPILOGUE

2001 – The Future?

As this book is published, Hackney Stadium stands derelict and abandoned. This is a crime. But with the current owners shrouded in secrecy, it's a little difficult to ascertain their plans. On the positive side, Hackney Council seem unwilling to allow the site to be redeveloped, telling prospective owners that the stadium must be retained as a sports arena. There are also rumours that dog racing is to return and that the site will become a new stadium, replacing plans to develop the old Lea Valley Park.

In 2001, a group of fans started a campaign to bring the sport back to Waterden Road. Two challenge matches were held at Rye House, which saw Barry Thomas make a one-off comeback, scoring 1 in the 30-60 defeat, and at Somerset where the Hawks won 46-42. A London Cup match was arranged at newly reopened Wimbledon for 2002, but that was scrapped and now it seems the campaign has fizzled out.

At this point, if Hackney is ever to return to being a speedway venue again, it will need a proper promoter – a known name with money behind him. It will also need a sympathetic stadium owner. Whilst the stadium still stands these two things are possible, but as yet there is no sign of that dream coming true.

We live in hope...

APPENDIX 1

THE HACKNEY TRACK RECORD

1935-1937   Division 1   Track Length 340 yards

Year	Track Record	Holder
1935 First Race	75.11	Dicky Case
1935	73.75	Dicky Case
1935	73.40	Ron Johnson
1935	72.03	Joe Francis
1935 End	71.65	Dicky Case
1936 End	70.60	Frank Charles
1937 End	70.50	Cordy Milne

1938-1939   Division 2   Track Length 340 yards

Year	Track Record	Holder
1938 Div. 2 record	72.76	Frank Hodgson
1938 End	72.2	Dug Wells
1939 End	71.2	Archie Windmill

In 1938 Max Grosskreutz clocked a time of 71.98, but this was disallowed as he was deemed to be of Division One standard.

1963-1983   Track Length 345 yards

Year	Track Record	Holder
1963 First Race	75.8	Tommy Sweetman
1963	72.2	Norman Hunter/Reg Reeves
1963	70.2	Colin Pratt
1963 End	70.0	Norman Hunter
1964	70.0	Norman Hunter/Colin Pratt
1964 End	69.2	Colin Pratt
1965	69.2	Colin Pratt/John Poyser/ Gerlad Jackson
1965	68.0	Colin Pratt
1965	67.2	Sverre Harrfeldt/Nigel Boocock
1965	66.8	Barry Briggs
1965 End	66.6	Barry Briggs
1966 End	66.4	Colin Pratt/ Barry Briggs
1967	66.4	Colin Pratt/ Barry Briggs/ Ivan Mauger
1967	66.2	Ivan Mauger/Colin Pratt
1967 End	66.0	Bob Kilby
1968 End	65.8	Colin Pratt/Barry Briggs/ Bengt Jansson/Nigel Boocock
1969 End	65.8	Colin Pratt/Barry Briggs/ Bengt Jansson/Nigel Boocock
1970 End	65.6	Ole Olsen
1971	65.0	Barry Thomas
1971 End	64.8	Garry Middleton/Ronnie Moore
1972 End	64.6	Barry Thomas
1973	64.4	Bengt Jansson
1973 End	64.2	Anders Michanek
1974 End	64.0	John Louis/Dave Jessup
1975 End	63.8	Ray Wilson/John Louis
1976	63.4	Tommy Jansson/Peter Collins
1976 End	63.0	Gordon Kennett
1977	63.0	Gordon Kennett/ Ole Olsen
1977	62.6	Keith White/Dave Jessup
1977 End	62.2	Ole Olsen
1978 End	62.2	Ole Olsen
1979 End	62.0	Zenon Plech/Finn Thomsen
1980 End	62.0	Zenon Plech/Finn Thomsen
1981	61.9	Tommy Knudsen
1981 End	61.8	Bruce Penhall/Bo Petersen
1982 End	61.3	Bo Petersen
1982	61.1	Michael Lee
1983 End	61.0	Bo Petersen

1984-1991   Track Length 320 yards

Year	Track Record	Holder
1984 First Race	65.8	Barry Thomas
1984	64.7	Barry Thomas
1984	63.9	Barry Thomas
1984	62. 8	Bob Garrad
1984 End	61.9	Martin Yeates/Kevin Teager
1985	61.8	Paul Whittaker
1985	61.7	Paul Whittaker
1985 End	61.2	Erik Gundersen
1986 End	61.2	Erik Gundersen/Kelvin Tatum
1987 End	60.0	Erik Gundersen
1988 End	60.0	Erik Gundersen
1989 End	60.0	Erik Gundersen
1990 End	59.5	Andy Galvin
1991 End	59.5	Andy Galvin

1995-1996   Track Length 301 metres

Year	Track Record	Holder
1995 Grand Prix	62.4	Jason Crump
1996	61.6	Jason Crump
1996	61.1	Peter Karlsson/Greg Hancock
1996	61.0	Leigh Adams
1996	60.6	Jason Crump
1996 End	59.8	Peter Karlsson

APPENDIX 2

THE LONDON CUP

While the London Riders Championship was the sport's oldest individual event, The London Cup is speedway's oldest team competition and was taken extremely seriously by London's speedway teams. In speedway's boom years, the majority of teams were in London and the cup was keenly fought between several teams on a knockout basis.

*Run on a league basis

Year	Winner
1930	Wembley beat Stamford Bridge
1931	Crystal Palace beat Wembley
1932	Wembley beat Stamford Bridge
1933	Wembley beat Wimbledon
1934	New Cross beat West Ham
1935	Harringay beat West Ham
1936	Hackney beat Harringay
1937	New Cross beat West Ham
1938	Wimbledon beat New Cross
1939	Wimbledon beat New Cross
1940-1945	No competition
1946	Wembley beat Wimbledon
1947	New Cross beat Wembley
1948	Wembley beat New Cross
1949	Wembley beat West Ham
1950	Wembley beat Wimbledon

Year	Winner
1951	Wembley beat Harringay
1952	Harringay beat Wimbledon
1953	Harringay beat West Ham
1954	Wembley beat Wimbledon
1955-1960	No competition
1961	Wimbledon beat New Cross
1962-1963	No competition
1964	Wimbledon beat West Ham
1965	West Ham *
1966	West Ham *
1967	West Ham *
1968	Wimbledon *
1969	Wimbledon *
1970	Wimbledon
1971	Hackney *
1972	Not held
1973	Hackney beat Wimbledon
1974	Wimbledon beat Hackney
1975	Wimbledon beat Hackney
1976	Wimbledon (run at Hackney only)
1977	White City *
1978	Wimbledon beat Hackney
1979	Hackney beat Wimbledon
1980	Wimbledon beat Hackney
1981	Hackney beat Wimbledon
1982	Wimbledon beat Hackney
1983	Wimbledon beat Hackney
1984	No competition
1985	Wimbledon beat Hackney
1986	Hackney beat Wimbledon
1987	Hackney beat Wimbledon
1988	Not held as both teams competed in the National League Cup final
1989	Hackney beat Wimbledon

APPENDIX 3

DID YOU KNOW?

West Ham pre-war star Eric Chitty was on occasion the Hackney Wolves announcer.

Dicky Case was once landlord of the Rye House Residential Hotel, which he took charge of as well as the speedway training school. Sadly, his wife was run over and killed on the bridge outside the pub.

During the pre-war years a band would play during the interval on the centre green, conducted by none other than Hackney's Dug Wells.

Hackney became the first track to stage a Christmas meeting on Boxing Day 1936. It was so popular that the event was repeated for the following two seasons, although the 1938 event was snowed off!

On several occasions the Hackney Supporters Club entered a float into the Tower Hamlets and Leyton Carnival.

How many people rang the stadium to see if a meeting had been rained off before travelling. Remember the number? 01 985 9822.

Apart from Haigh, Harding, Pyeatt and Muchene, a fifth rider junior, Alan Clegg, was killed at the Hackney training school in January 1972.

Both Malcolm Brown and Keith White released songs called 'Speedway'.

In the home match against West Ham on 11 May 1969, a surprise and secret guest was Prince Rainier of Monaco. Apparently he had visited Waterden Road before the war and, on discovering it was still operational, had requested a return visit.

The Hackney pits have been situated in four different places. Pre-war, the pits were on the first bend at the end of the main grandstand. On reopening in 1963 the pits were behind the main grandstand before being moved in 1967 to the fourth bend, where they remained until closure in 1991. In 1995 the new stadium had temporary pits on the site of the old fourth bend pits for the Grand Prix, but for the following season's league matches the pits were directly in front of the main stand.

Barry Sheene once rode a speedway bike at the Hackney training school.

Colin Pratt's only riding appearance at Hackney following the Lokeren Road tragedy was in a promoters' race on 30 October 1977. Pratt won, beating Bob Dugard, Cyril Maidment and Len Silver.

In 1984, a team called Hackney 83 won a four-team event at Arena Essex by scoring 32 points and beating both Cradley and Oxford in the process. Bo Petersen scored 11, Finn Thomsen 8.

Berwick's Bruce Cribb once gave an interval ice-racing demonstration. He took his ice-racing bike around Waterden Road in a time of 57.2, the conventional track record being 61.9.

Dicky Case with Hackney's first ever trophy, the 1936 London Cup (see Appendix 2).

The Hackney Supporters' Club carnival float (see Appendix 3).

Len 'Mc'Silver

An aerial view of the Hackney stadium.